"Saying 'no' to a misbehavior is entirely different than saying 'no' to feelings. This important and practical book teaches parents how to do that."

—John Bradshaw, author of *Homecoming*
and *Healing the Shame That Binds You*

"Who would have thought so much could be said about a two letter word? This book is must reading for parents and will enrich your relationship with your child in ways that will change you and your child forever.

—Garry L. Landreth, Regents Professor and Director,
Center for Play Therapy, University of North Texas

"Mark Brenner's book is a must-read for parents who are tired of saying 'no' to their children and tired of what isn't working. This book can change your child's behavior!

—Mark Goulston, M.D.,
Assistant Clinical Professor of Psychology, UCLA

"The best book about limit-setting I have ever read. I'd like to make this 'required reading' for every parent."

—Pediatrician Jay Gordon, M.D.

"Chock-full of practical good advice for concerned parents. My advice is to read it and apply it now!"

—Albert Pizzo, M.D.

WHEN "NO" GETS YOU NOWHERE

REVISED SECOND EDITION

Teaching Your Toddler
and Child Self-Control

Mark L. Brenner

PRIMA PUBLISHING

Copyright © 2001 by Mark L. Brenner

Published by Prima Publishing, Roseville, California. Member of the Crown Publishing
Group, a division of Random House, Inc.

Random House, Inc. New York, Toronto, London, Sydney, Auckland

PRIMA PUBLISHING and colophon are trademarks of Random House, Inc., regis-
tered with the United States Patent and Trademark Office.

"Children Will Listen" music and lyrics by Stephen Sondheim (from *Into the Woods*),
1988, 1993 Rilting Music, Inc. All rights administered by WB Music Corp. All rights re-
served. Used by permission of Warner Bros. Publications U.S. Inc., Miami, FL 33014.
Quotes from *Teacher and Child* by Dr. Haim Ginott (Collier Books, 1993) and
Between Parent and Child by Dr. Haim Ginott (Avon, 1969) used by permission of Dr.
Alice Ginott.

Library of Congress Cataloging-in-Publication Data on File
  ISBN 0-7615-3480-6

01 02 03 04 HH 10 9 8 7 6 5 4 3 2 1
Printed in the United States of America

Second Edition

Visit us online at www.primapublishing.com

To the memory of Haim G. Ginott.

Contents

Preface

The Legacy of Dr. Haim G. Ginott

It's been more than 40 years since the works of Dr. Haim Ginott were first published, and they continue to pass the test of time that history demands, remaining classic and timeless. His body of work in child development and his methods of communicating are brilliantly straightforward and incisive. He has influenced millions of people to understand the nature of, as well as the solutions to, relationships between the parent and child and between the teacher and student. His body of work on play and group therapy offers expert guidelines and insights to the process of individual and group psychotherapy. It was a great loss to the professional community, as well as to his family, students, and patients, when Haim Ginott died on November 4, 1973. His legacy and body of work will be taught for generations.

In his two books (written over 30 years ago), *Between Parent and Child* and *Between Parent and Teenager,* Ginott captured the full range of common patterns of behaviors as well as solutions that remain a blueprint for millions of parents.

The origins of behavior and the nature of man in his search for meaning are mystically and purposefully elusive. Still, at the end of that journey man must talk with man. Ginott understood this and dedicated his life to the principles of communication between man and child. He identified what he called "self-defeating patterns of behavior" and offered new ideas to conquer them.

Like all the great masters, he was a pioneer in his field of the human sciences. Our children are our last and best hope for humanity. Ginott's work has influenced that hope.

Acknowledgments

To Georgia Hughes, my first editor at Prima Publishing, who saw the original manuscript and said, "You've got a book here"—thank you. Also, thank you to Jamie Miller and her team at Prima for continuing to believe in the message of *When "No" Gets You Nowhere* and suggesting a revised edition.

To my mother, for her unwavering belief in me throughout my life and reminding me every few years that I should write and teach.

To Rae and Jack Gindi, who have influenced my life in so many positive ways and who have always been champions for "the children." A belated thank you to Mel Gotlieb for his wise guidance.

To Judah Klausner and our shared experiences for respecting the inner world of children.

To Lisa Weil for her straightforward comments about this subject, seventeen years of selfless contributions to elementary school education, and loyal friendship. To my closest friend and brother Elie Gindi, who embodies the essence of friendship.

To Dr. Albert Pizzo and my early days at The Children's Neurological Clinic, and all the parents and children who showed me the enormous potential and capacity for human development. To Garry Landreth, whose work has quietly touched my life personally and professionally.

To my beautiful wife Penny, whose love and devotion to our family made writing this book so easy and natural.

Finally, to my son Max and my daughter Merrill, who show me every day a new meaning for everything!

Introduction:
Why This Book?

ALL THE KING'S horses and all the king's men couldn't put Humpty Dumpty together again. Five-minute remedies, 1-minute cures, and weekend workshops—these are the promises of the self-help, quick-fix prophets. Truth is, there are no 5=minute remedies, especially when it comes to parenting. Beware. The pendulum reflecting family conflicts has swung far from its center arc, but it will return. At the same time, new emerging family structures have gone way beyond the blended and traditional extended family lifestyles to give rise to an even more complex environment.

Sadly and understandably, parents today are more frustrated and confused about when and how to say "no" to their children during their early childhood development than perhaps any other time in the last 75 years. Parents are acknowledging that just being a loving parent is oftentimes not enough. This book presents alternative thinking to saying "no" while at the same time setting limits to teach a child self-control. In that context, I hope that fewer children-turned-adults will have to recall the Humpty Dumpty tale, asking a psychologist, "Can you put me together again?"

While writing this book, a friend of mine asked me a question about why his 3-year-old doesn't comply when he says no! When I gave him the answer he said, "Wow, you would have to be a psychologist!" I knew exactly what he meant. I had a similar experience when my wife and I were planning for our infant son's first series of immunizations. I spoke with someone I knew who was well read on the subject of immunizations. When he gave me his recommendation, I said, "Wow, you would have to be a doctor!" I have consciously remembered that parallel experience and have come to the conclusion that your instinct to ask the right questions will lead you to the right answers.

Just the fact that you're thinking about buying this book (or already have) shows your interest in asking the right questions. The single question most parents ask is, "What's the one thing I can do that will have the biggest positive impact on my child's behavior?" I usually say, "Other than having your child see a loving marriage or a balanced healthy parent, it is to always acknowledge and allow your child the freedom to express his or her feelings without censorship!" Saying "no" to a child's feelings is very different than saying "no" to his or her misbehavior. Just as a vaccine can immunize the body, allowing the expression of feelings can immunize the human spirit. It has been my experience that many parents believe if they allow their children to express all their feelings, their behavior will automatically escalate to become more obnoxious and aggressive. Actually, the opposite is true. *If children can't say it out loud, they will act it out!* Feelings are at the epicenter of a their development.

If a child is genuinely respected for his feelings (even if you don't like what he is expressing), he will want to obey and abide by you more often. At the same time, parents, too, have feelings that need to be expressed at the appropriate moment. This is also how children learn to express their emotions at the right time. When a child pushes too hard to extend his limits, the parent should feel free to honestly express his or her anger. "Darren, Daddy is angry! (Pausing) You drew all over the couch with the pen. I'm very, very upset! You know the pen is only for paper. This makes me very angry!" Don't be afraid to let your child hear and feel these emotional consequences. However, never degrade, humiliate, or compare him to anyone else when you express your anger. If you express your anger through feelings, he will be far more encouraged to learn how to channel his own emotions as well as learn self-control. Constantly saying no to misbehavior without providing a reason will heighten conflict. This is not to say we need to get permission when we put our foot down, but the bigger picture is the bigger lesson—teaching a child to think first. That is why the way you give information to a child will, in the end, be the determining factor in shaping his behavior and responses.

Most parenting books today on child psychology share a point of view reflecting more about what is politically popular in our society than what is psychologically healthy behavior for our children to be participating in. I've always maintained that just as there's a difference between being physically fit and physically healthy, there is a difference between being a loving parent and being a healthy parent.

When "No" Gets You Nowhere reveals new ways to build your child's trust in you and self-control in him or herself. This is not a book on permissiveness; it is a book about selectiveness. It examines the effects of a child hearing the word no or feeling its equivalency through constant physical expressions such as grabbing, lifting, or taking objects away. This book shows that most of what we're saying "no" to interferes with the more important lesson: the building of trust between the parent and child, and the opportunity for the child to stop himself *first,* before his transgression

This may sound like a license for overindulgence. However, as you will soon discover, nothing could be farther from the truth. Basically, there are three categories of reasons of why we may have to say "no" to a child: the possibility of danger, stopping a misbehavior, or denying a request. If you want to fast-forward to see the 7-Step Method for Saying "No" in action, turn to chapter 8. However, if you want to understand the context behind these methods and why they work, try not to skip chapters and read this book from the beginning.

Stages of Development

THE FIRST five years are for life. That is, they take us through life. They are the blueprint for how we will be. In this regard, parents are responsible for helping shape the emotional behavior patterns that children carry through life. To help support that process, it's important for parents to recognize and understand which stage of development their child is in. This will allow parents to connect the right message for setting limits and saying "no" with their child's feelings and behavior. As the title of this book implies, there's much more to know than just saying "no."

While many popular parenting books focus on what to expect developmentally, this book focuses on how to communicate when having to say "no" to misbehaviors during infancy, toddlerhood, and childhood. After you have read these ideas and begin to examine your own relationship with your child, you will quickly discover that knowing how and when to say "no" will dramatically minimize your child's need for acting out and having tantrums. You will learn how to lessen what others have comfortably declared "normal" or "only a stage."

It is common for parents to seek professional help after they have exhausted numerous approaches to correct a child's constant misbehaviors. Although the field of child psychology has long kept secret its tools for changing behavior, these ideas are now making their way to the forefront of parent-child education. I have always believed that parents are, in fact, the ideal agents for change when they are given the proper tools and communication principles. In a relatively short period of time, parents too can begin to reverse patterns of problem behavior that otherwise would have been left to the professional.

A Note About the Use of Pronouns

The English language sometimes makes it difficult to follow whether an author is referring to a child who is male or female. To help solve this problem, I have randomly alternated the use of *he* and *she*. Please understand that while writing this book, it was my intention for you to have your own child in mind.

A Boy in the Game

He stands at the plate, with heart pounding fast,
The bases are loaded; his focus must last.

Mom and Dad cannot help him; he stands all alone,
A hit right now, would send the team home.
The ball crosses the plate; he swings and he misses,

There's a groan from the crowd, with some boos and some hisses.
A thoughtless voice shouts, "Strike the punk out!"
Tears fill his eyes; his bat weighed a ton,

Something had changed, the game's no longer fun.
For it's moments like this; a man you can make,
Keep this in mind, when you guide a boy's fate.

And if you're not sure, what this all means
Remember the "shout" that cast a certain doubt.
Words can be weapons, and hit hard like a fist,
Next time think twice, before you're remiss.

—M B

What to Know About Saying "No"

For an infant, toddler, or child, rarely does the word *no* just mean stop! It's a small word that carries with it big emotional consequences. Most words or expressions that are overused eventually lose their power and meaning. Not so with the word *no*. You will soon see when children are bombarded with hearing the word *no*, its negative effects are cumulative and become more significant and ubiquitous over time. It' s a simple word that carries multiple subtle meanings that will follow a child outside his or her home, from classroom to classroom to every aspect of life.

Human competitiveness, parenting reprimands, family conflicts, and intense peer pressures will remind each child what they have been told all too often by others. Soon the word takes on a new meaning and context, in effect saying, "No you can't do that, but I can!" This is not a book about self-esteem or the effects of saying "no" on a child's self-worth. It's not a book about how-to discipline. It is a book about teaching toddlers and children inner self-control by the way in which we tell them "no" and, more importantly, how we act when they inevitably do transgress.

We teach that process by having children watch our own behavior and listen to our words. If the only time we used the word "no" was to stop a child from a potentially dangerous situation, then the point of this book would be moot. In 1930, the psychologist E. Lee Vincent said that parents should give children discipline in such a way as "to direct human behavior without injuring the human being."

Listen carefully to how many times a day someone says "no" to your child. Listen for the subtle nuances that say "No, that's wrong!" or "No, you can't!" In his book *First Feelings,* child psychiatrist Stanley Greenspan suggests how parents may unwittingly interfere too soon in a toddler's play or exploration by showing her a better or faster way to do something. For the toddler who has not yet signaled for help (through visual frustration), this unnecessary interference sends the signal, "You're doing it wrong!" You can see how, without the word *no* ever being used, such interference would be internalized as though the word *no* had been spoken, regardless of the parents' good intentions. Even though the parent may have taken the toy to show her a better way, the child perceives the act of it being taken as a power struggle and a form of punishment. There is a huge difference between interaction and interference.

By needlessly saying the word *no* throughout the day to express our disapproval, we are exponentially increasing this communicative dosage. One example of this kind of premature interference centers around 18-month-old Jason, who was learning to play with a new electronic toy that worked by matching sounds with places (animals in a zoo, water in the ocean, and so forth). Jason was able to clumsily press the buttons to hear the different sounds, but his mother was unhappy with the way he did it. She wanted him to correctly match the sounds with the places so he would have a "better" learning experience. The mother seemed more preoccupied with the fact that he wasn't using the toy the "right way" than in noticing Jason's overall learning experience and pleasure from simply pressing the buttons successfully, smiling to the different sounds, and watching the toy move. Pretty soon his mother's frequent control over "playing the right way" with other toys became a symbol for power struggles over the daily routines of napping, changing, and eating. It was as though little Jason was saying, "If she won't let me be the 'chief' some of the time with my toys, then I will be the 'chief' in other ways."

This is yet another example where an 18- or 20-month-old doesn't hear the literal word *no*, but rather feels it through the parent's attitude and unintended interference. That's not to say that if you sometimes interfere too quickly in your child's play, you' re doing damage. You're not! It also doesn't mean your child will grow up insecure or feeling incompetent. However, a parent's continuing controlling interference during a child's play or activities *will* result in greater daily parent-child conflict. In other words, *you* become the target.

> A parent's continuing controlling interference during a child's play or activities *will* result in greater daily parent-child conflict. In other words, *you* become the target.

Perhaps it's ironic that all toddlers pass through a fierce "saying no" phase that reflects the intensity and duration of how and when we say "no" to them. Unable to stop this automatic response, parents know and feel self-conscious about sometimes reacting too heavy-handed when disciplining their child. More often, those controlling reactions become blurred and the parents' actions are forgotten years later should the child become successful in life. When this happens, a parent may say to others, "You see, those things didn't matter anyway."

I am reminded of the story of Robert, a 4-year-old boy who was subjected to a very unsympathetic home life and was perpetually bombarded by a condescending attitude from his parents. Being told "no" was as commonplace as his rebellious actions toward both his parents and the world. His parents communicated with him in such a way that Robert felt incompetent and untrustworthy. "No. Put that back, you're going to break it!" "No. You can't go." "How many times do I have to tell you? No, that's not yours!" In response, Robert's temper tantrums grew louder and more random with time. As an adult he cleverly masked his anger, verbally striking out at others where fewer eyes could see. Still, years later at the age of 47, Robert managed to become a very successful executive. In the process of masking their real resentment, some people, like Robert, learn early on how to cleverly compensate for those haunting residual feelings. Though some of these people do achieve great success, they often carry great personal pain that always spills over into their personal relationships. As long as we value power and winning over emotional maturity, the umbrella and mystique of success will spin those unflattering personality behaviors into symbols of triumph and role models for others to follow who are less insightful to notice the real problem. Unfortunately, more common are those adults who were unsuccessful in escaping these early problems and subsequently unable to climb out of that pain to achieve their full potential.

Up to this point I have made a deliberate attempt to avoid providing substitute language for the word *no*. I feel it is necessary to establish the context of the word and show it first as a concept than as a simple word to stop a particular behavior. The word by itself is far too limiting and therefore this book looks for ways to expand and clarify its meaning and impact; in other words, to find more effective ways to encourage a child to stop himself before he loses it, or—just as common—before the parent does. There are no words that when said all the time, work all the time. What *will* work all the time is understanding the principles behind *When "No" Gets You Nowhere!*

One of these principles is to first give your child the opportunity to act correctly rather than your just abruptly stopping a misbehavior (other than a dangerous activity). For example, a 2-year-old spilling a bag of potato chips on the floor can be told, "Todd, I see you want to put the potato chips on the floor, but they belong in the bag. I know you understand that!" This response should be said *before* taking the potato chips away (or helping put them back), which gives the toddler a moment of time to make the connection and act accordingly. What should be avoided is just shouting, "No, don't do that!" Naturally, in the beginning it's highly unlikely the toddler will abide and hand the bag of remaining potato chips to his parent. What *is* highly likely over time is the child's diminished need to test that parent. In the end, it's the parent's attitude, mood, and facial cues when providing the straightforward information about where something belongs that allow the toddler a chance to think about his behavior. This process takes the focus away from the potential conflict between the parent and the child. Of course, a toddler's dangerous actions such as hitting or running out of control in public must always be stopped immediately. However, even then the child must be told in a way whereby the lesson is heard, learned, and remembered so the child remains safe.

Parents should also try to remain realistic about how long it will take for a toddler to learn to control himself. If our expectations are more in line with what is realistic, then our constant reminders (without using the word *no*) won't seem so tiresome and unexpected. Somehow we mistakenly think to ourselves, "Maybe this time will be the last." In time, and with lots of patience, your child will learn to self-regulate through this mindful process. We need to be diligent about not giving him more reasons to rebel than his own natural expressions for independence call for. If a parent sets and communicates concrete limits and gives straightforward information—without resorting to personal attacks—about why something is unacceptable, a toddler, sooner rather than later, will abide more often. These principles, in stark contrast to your immediately grabbing something back or saying negative expressions such as "No, that's not for you!" or "Henry, how many times do I have to tell you?" will help encourage your child to abide by you more often. Initially, most toddlers and children are looking for both acknowledgment (without shame) of their feelings and straightforward information about how to solve the problem.

> If a parent sets and communicates concrete limits and gives straightforward information about why something is unacceptable without resorting to personal attacks, a toddler will abide more often.

Why Saying "No" Doesn't Work

IT'S IMPORTANT to understand why saying the word *no* doesn't work. A child's misbehavior or badness has two parts: The first part is his actions and the second is his feelings. As child psychologist Dorothy Baruch wrote: "His feelings are the cause and his actions are the result." This must be recognized if we are to change our understanding as well as our child's behavior.

In their everyday manner of relating to children, parents sometimes deal only with the misbehavior, ignoring the child's feelings: "Alex, I'm warning you," or "I don't care if you are mad, you're going anyway." At the other extreme are those parents who sometimes go too far and can turn a moment into a therapy session, asking their 3-year-old, "Why are you so mean to your brother?" Although the parent's intent to learn about his or her child's anger is good, a young toddler or a 5-year-old child is not capable of saying, "Well Mom, I believe it is just sibling rivalry." A better response from the parent is, "Bobby, I see how angry you are at your brother. You don't want to share your toys with him now. It makes you angry when he takes them!" Genuine acknowledgment of his feelings will diminish his need to be mean over time. The expression of feelings by the child without personal judgments from the parent will create the psychological value that makes disciplining the child easier. Simply put, "bad feelings" bring about "bad actions." The focus of this book is not what makes children difficult or mean, but rather what makes them *better*. That is why we do not hit children when we want them to stop hitting. We do not yell at children to get them to stop yelling. We do not call them names to get them to stop calling other people names. And we do not throw fits to get them to stop throwing fits.

Why Do We Say "No" So Quickly?

FEW THINGS take only one minute. Saying "no" properly in the beginning takes time. Time must be allowed for the parent's explanation and the child's reaction to the disappointment (with the parent accepting the child's need to complain). Most important, time must be allowed for the child to transgress before prematurely taking an action. Parents must be careful not to preempt a child's potential misbehavior by saying, "Ah, ah, ah . . . Carol, remember, I'm watching you!" This only serves to tell your child you have no confidence in her and are expecting her to do wrong. It will feel like "gotcha." The brilliant Fred (Mr.) Rogers said it best: "Being supportive often means waiting and listening, and more waiting, until you're better able to understand the drama that a certain child is living through at the moment."

Saying "no" properly can take 30 seconds or 5 minutes, depending upon how long you've practiced these principles and what the circumstances are. These combinations of interactions between the parent and child are the foundation for mutual respect, which translates to a child's desire to abide. Don't mistake this process as appearing to be too soft or empowering. You can be strong and unbending, and still respectful. Common responses from most parents who hurl "no" commands at their children early on are, "I want them to know they have limits," "I don't want to spoil them," or "I want to protect them from something dangerous." These are all worthwhile lessons, but there is another lesson: the wisdom of knowing how and when to intervene. Those moments of mindfulness will translate to helping build a newfound trust between parent and child.

The frequency of using the word *no* and the building of trust have a direct relationship with each other. There is a right time for intervention, interaction, and observation. Still many parents say "no" like a reflex without really thinking it through. They do this for many reasons:

1. The parent is either too tired or wants to do something else and ignores the child's questions and curiosity.

2. The parent has no patience to understand the real meaning behind the child's behavior. As child psychologist Haim Ginott said, "Children talk in code;" although they may verbalize one intent, their private feelings are often completely different.

3. All too commonly, the parents' own impatient and neurotic frustrations cause them to appear out of control (the combination of having been overprotected or overdisciplined by their own parents may be one reason for their own outbursts). More often than not, these reactions from parents become almost automatic. That is why some adults find themselves saying, "I can't believe it! I am talking and acting with my child the way my parents did with me!"

A toddler or child will learn self-control faster if he sees it first in his parents.

2

Saying "No"
Too Soon

T HE WORD *NO* is arguably the most overused, negatively applied word in the parenting repertoire. Almost from day one (straight from the hospital), some parents believe this is the word, the only word, that will teach and stop behavior. They carry the word with them like a weapon, feeling prepared, confident, and ready to protect.

"No, don't put that in your mouth."
"No, don't touch that."
"No, don't go near that."
"No, that's not for you."

Parents should understand that saying the word *no* frequently and too early to infants has little or no positive value in their development. As a matter of fact, over time it can diminish enthusiasm and curiosity. If you're concerned about an infant touching something dangerous, it's best to pick the child up and place him or her somewhere safer. Don't make a moment an event! Just acknowledge what your child is looking at and quietly change his or her direction. "I see you want to touch the stapler."

Cooing or shouting the word *no* can confuse or startle infants because they do not connect hearing "no" with their own specific behaviors. Although some parents intuit their infant's confusion, they sometimes still feel compelled to say the word *no*. To allow for stronger development, parents should encourage uninterrupted curiosity, which can also lead to a healthier spirit and temperament. For an infant, early impulses to crawl in a certain direction are the first signs of self-motivation. Parents should be prepared to allow this behavior and development to occur before saying and teaching the meaning of "no."

Two-year-olds, however, will react to hearing the word *no* completely differently. They won't be startled. They will be challenged! Their level of trust in what you say and the understanding they have of what you're saying "no" to will diminish their need to challenge. A better alternative to saying "no" is to just give the information without making a personal judgment or attack on personality. "Nancy, the spoon belongs on the table," or "Jacob, this is a ketchup bottle. Ketchup is inside. The cap belongs on the bottle." Continuous reminders through information will achieve a better result in stopping a misbehavior or a potential misbehavior.

You must first, however, recognize that toddlerhood is a unique stage, behaving, as psychologist E. H. Erikson says, "with limitless self-extension." Toddlers want to be everywhere, to freely examine, explore, and hunt—all with a fiery spirit of "I can do things!" Here the parent should exercise his or her judgment of when and when not to intervene.

Their Home Is Their Laboratory

OUTSIDE OF imminent or potential danger (see chapter 6), infants and young toddlers should be allowed to touch, pick up, taste, or drop objects without intervention or interruption. Their home is their laboratory. This is their primary environment, which should provide a sense of safety and confidence about exploring.

Of course you must always keep a watchful eye. The wisdom of knowing when to intervene is the key here. For example, does scratching the screen door with their fingers or playing with the guard gate require intervention or observation? These are the early stages when your infant-turned-toddler begins to notice your trust in him by what you're willing to let him do. (It goes without saying that expensive or favorite family objects should be put away during this stage!) When a toddler reaches for a new object, just supervise his behavior. Let him see your patience and trust. Many parents say, "I can't let my infant or toddler throw things"; "I can't let her run free"; "She has to learn now to respect things." She will. The timing to teaching such lessons is key. Let's look at some of these concerns realistically, one at a time.

> Toddlerhood is a unique stage. Toddlers want to be everywhere, to freely examine, explore, and hunt—all with a fiery spirit of "I can do things!"

First, infants 7 to 9 months old are not running around throwing things. They're crawling around. There are no lessons yet to be taught in self-discipline. Their lessons are all in self-discovery. Second, for toddlers there is a difference between running free and feeling free. This is an especially difficult stage due to the constant state of alertness a parent must maintain. One mother with twins calls it "active watching." At this age, toddlers seem to physically put themselves in the middle of new situations, wanting to manage the outcome. Third, toddlers will learn to respect an object after they learn "how things work." They transform, manipulate, and combine whatever objects or materials may be in their hands. Symbolically, they are shaping and exploring themselves.

Everything is an experiment within an experiment. At another time and stage, after they have freely experienced this process, they will show the more accepted expression of respect by "taking care of things." Again, everything is age and stage related.

Readiness Is Everything

WHEN TODDLERS experience something for the first or even second time, they don't always require immediate parental commentary, whether it be simple or complex ("Look, Carol, let Daddy show you how it works"). They are discovering and developing their own inner commentary and process. Just watching a 2-year-old's face as he looks at something new will reveal to you just how focused his mind is. As Dr. Arnold Gesell, an early pioneer in child development, says, "The mind manifests itself." In other words, intelligence will advance at its own pace and will be utilized and maximized within the child's emotional readiness. That is why you will sometimes see children not working to their potential. Emotional maturity and the link between how a child feels about himself many times determine his outward progress.

When parents consistently interfere too quickly in their child's play, they are sending the message, "You can't do it, you need help." In turn, the child may feel helpless. Solution: Look for their cue first. Likewise, a child who continues to signal for help after being frustrated and then does not receive it may wind up abandoning that activity altogether. This kind of pattern can lead to a child not wanting to complete tasks and moving from one activity to another. Even a 3-year-old would rather appear as if he doesn't want to do something rather than being unable to do something. Armed with this kind of understanding, you can now better read your child's expression that says, "I need help or an explanation *now!*" Timing is everything.

Imagine being on a tour where you see the breathtaking Grand Canyon for the first time. You think to yourself, "Wow, look at it, it's amazing," and seconds later you are bombarded through a loudspeaker with statistical and geological information. What an interruption! The information is useful, but it comes at the wrong time; the observing experience should come first. It is the same for your toddler. Whether you're visiting friends, at the park, or watching her play with your shoes in the closet, your toddler sees things that can totally engage her focus of attention. She will signal you for help or an explanation when she is ready. You can see it all over her face. The toddler years are precisely what life is all about—discovery and experience!

It' s natural to want our children to develop quickly. Number one, it is easier to take care of them when they're older, and number two, the feeling of being able to mutually exchange dialogue is very rewarding. However, unless we provide a more tolerant environment, we may be putting them at risk for developmental difficulties. This can be seen in any stage of development but is most obvious in late infancy or early toddlerhood.

Have you ever put grass seed down on newly turned soil? What does it require to grow? Water and sunshine, of course, but the big factor is allowing time for the roots to mature. We never say after a week, "This would be a good time to test it; let's walk through it now." We must remind ourselves that infancy and early toddlerhood are a child's time to exclusively and endlessly explore. Then, at a later time, he will be more trusting with you and ready to understand the behavioral lessons that will take him through life.

Two Stories That Speak Volumes

A BEAUTIFUL and very alert 9-month-old girl was just beginning to learn to sit up at a local park. I watched her as my son was playing in a large sandbox only a few feet from her. It was autumn and a golden leaf blew up in the air and landed right in front of her. She looked at it intensely and was as pleased as if someone had just put a toy in front of her. After examining the leaf for about one minute, she reached for the leaf with her hand and drew it close, ready to feel the crisp texture and weight, smell its scent, and yes, maybe taste her first fall season, when . . . BAM! the mother lunged in front of her and grabbed the leaf from her hand, saying, "Tammy, no good. It's not for your mouth. No, no, it's bad for you," and instead replaced the leaf with a plastic toy. "Here, Tammy, a rattle."

Needless to say, the toy was dropped almost instantly with a limp sadness. Tammy knew she had just held something more interesting! This true anecdote speaks volumes to parents who see the wisdom in knowing how and when to say "no." An alternative approach would be to let the infant either play with the leaf or taste it (children learn fast when something doesn't taste good), or to simply explain where the leaf belongs without making the leaf "bad." Perhaps a better response to the above scenario would be something along the lines of, "Tammy, leaves belong on the ground. They may be dirty because people and animals walk on them." In general, the words *good* and *bad* should be reserved for moral issues, not daily behavior and reminders. Children hear these words differently and may totalize all their behavior in relation to what you are saying (see chapter 4).

Angela, just 9 months old, was crawling to the dog bowl to take a closer look at what was inside when her mother said, "No, no, that's not for you. That's the dog's, honey." Angela's harmless little excursion was abruptly cut short by her mom, who ignored the smile and enthusiasm Angela was bringing on her way to the bowl. This was far more important than the information that the food was for the dog. At 9 months old she couldn't identify whose food this was. Angela's focus was on her new mobility and excitement. If her mother didn't want her to touch the dog food, she could have said, "I know you see the dog food," and gently placed her somewhere else.

The message *should* have been, "Yes, Angela, you can see everything and crawl anywhere!" Remember, don't make a moment an event. As a parent, you can best understand your child by trying to see through her lens and recognizing that her play is really her work! What is the harm in most infant or toddler explorations? Opening up jars, spilling cereal on the floor, going through Mommy's pocketbook—these are expected. Touching a sliced tomato—perfect! Tasting a newspaper—mmmm! Opening up a drawer—the jackpot! The point is, that's your child's job now. Your job is to watch him do it and let him see your trust. Then calmly comment about where something belongs or help identify an object. "Tommy, cereal belongs in the bowl." "Newspapers are for reading, not for the mouth." You may ask, Where's the discipline?

> As a parent, you can best understand your child by trying to see through her lens and recognizing that her play is really her work!

Like all behavior, sometimes it requires observation, other times intervention, and still other times interaction.

The first 15 months should be considered a child's rite of passage, and parents should try not to interrupt the physical expression of curiosity. They do all the work, you do all the cleanup! True, it takes enormous patience, a watchful eye, and an unbelievable attitude, but isn't that what you promised yourself you would do? Your patience will speak volumes as you prepare for your toddler' s next stage: sentence and vocabulary expansion.

Remember, you are building the most important foundation in parenting: mutual trust. The first 15 months are about your child's exploration and discovering his own experimental powers.

3

"No, It's Mine!"

"Alex, give Daddy the remote control, please."
"No, it's mine!"

"Shannon, let the little boy play with the toy."
"No, it's mine!"

"Becky, can I . . ."
"No, it's mine!"

I F THESE CUTE signs of independence turned quickly to cooperation, we would all laugh with relief. However, when an object is taken from a toddler, the more common reaction is an outburst. The intensity of the outburst, ranging from a momentary whimper to a full-fledged screaming, kicking tantrum, is measured and tracked in large part by a child's previous experiences with you.

At the same time, this stage of "it's mine" will develop automatically with all toddlers. The difference is duration: when a 20-month-old realizes his new mobility can get him somewhere faster or that he can hold an object very tightly or grab a toy from another child, he will want to test his powers of fearlessness. A child will say, "No, it's mine." Sometimes it's playful, sometimes it's true, and sometimes he's just being mean-spirited. However, if parents pay particular attention to their choice of words, as well the timing of their intervention timing, this stage can be dramatically lessened in duration.

Looking Back

IF WE were able to look through the eyes of a toddler during the first 18 months of his life, we would most likely encounter his parents, brothers, sisters, or caregivers taking, grabbing, or pulling things away (gently or otherwise) every day. To compound this physical behavior, the family reinforces their reprimands with what I call "ownership messages" such as, "No, this is Daddy's phone," "No, this is Mommy's brush," "No, this is your sister's toy," "No, this is the dog's food." This approach overemphasizes possession. After hearing these expressions hundreds of times, the toddler is now convinced *everybody* has more than he does. A better approach would be, "Let's put the phone back on the table," or "Let's put the brush back in the drawer." These statements show no emphasis of ownership. At this stage it's not important who owns the object, but rather where it belongs.

Many parents, for various reasons, including wanting to avoid being embarrassed by their child, believe the magical age of somewhere between 15 and 20 months is the right time to teach their child the meaning of sharing. Unfortunately, a toddler's understanding of this concept is nonexistent and thus his reaction is one of confusion. "Tammy, will you share this?" Not surprisingly, Tammy answers, "No, it's mine."

If, however, you have built trust with your toddler in the first 18 months by allowing her to explore more freely ("I see you want to know what is in the drawer"), then, beginning at around 24 months, your toddler's experience with learning about sharing will be more relaxed and meaningful. Though she still may say,

"No, it's mine," the act of sharing will tie more into her natural development and less into a learned behavior. Later her need to prove "It's mine" will develop into her need to share.

Is Sharing Natural or Is It Learned?

TO SOME degree, sharing (like one's temperament) is an inherent quality. Some children naturally are givers. To a much larger extent sharing is learned. Teaching a 2-year-old to share too early has no meaning. Although some parents feel embarrassed when their toddlers are not prepared to share, they should try not to be. After all, it's not a reflection on them. As Patricia Shimm explains in her book *Parenting Your Toddler,* which is based on her work for 20 years at the Toddler Center at Barnard College in New York, "The concept [of sharing] is too advanced for most toddlers because they truly don't understand that all possessions shouldn't belong to them."

Socialization skills take place a little further into their development. Beginning at around 2 years of age, it is my belief that the way to introduce the concept is through descriptive feelings: "I see Bobby is not finished playing with the shovel yet. When he is finished, he will give it to you," or "I see you like to play alone with the shovel." These subtle expressions over many months will help diffuse power struggles, allowing the toddler to see the benefits of sharing—namely, making friends.

Why do so many children react differently when they are taught to share and what can we do to encourage it? The answer, as in the case of most behavior, lies within family systems as well as on the timing and pressure put upon a child to share.

Parents who consistently intervene too quickly and grab objects away from their children in an attempt to teach sharing are doing little to encourage the behavior they desire to see. Children, like adults, must come to their own insights in order for the right behavior to become permanent. Parents must truly respect this process if real and mature learning is to take place. No adult can ever force a child's readiness to give generously—the child must be emotionally ready. Experience is still our greatest teacher! Even 11-month-old infants can feel and give their trust when exchanging objects with a parent. The manner in which infants hold onto something and the manner in which they let go are both due in large part to the trusting relationship between the parent and child.

In the earlier examples with Tammy, the 9-month-old infant who picked the leaf up from the ground, or the 18-month-old who was stripped of the newspaper he had in his hand, a different lesson was learned: When you have something in your hand, better hold it tight, otherwise someone will try to take it! A parent's generous spirit in allowing exploration can oftentimes lessen such feelings and reactions.

> Children, like adults, must come to their own insights in order for the right behavior to become permanent. Parents must truly respect this process if real and mature learning is to take place.

This is not to suggest that parents who don't allow their toddlers access to their personal closets or dresser drawers will impart a negative influence on their child. They won't. However, continual restricting expressions and actions will reinforce and prepare an infant-turned-toddler for a more closed response to you and the world when he is ready to talk or asked to share.

It's no secret that a child's home is his most influential environment (see chapter 2). This is where he first views all social expressions, including sharing. Parents who are very restrictive in allowing their child to explore in their own home are also sending the message "These are my things and I don't want to share them with you." This fuels the toddler's selfishness and need to say "It's mine" longer. Parents must be prepared to think about such implications if they want to cultivate the values of sharing and generosity. It takes enormous patience and a great attitude to maintain your commitment to these principles. Child psychologist Charles E. Schaefer makes the following point: "Parents, for example, who refuse to put away their valuable glassware because they feel 2-year-old Jimmy must learn to respect their belongings are not respecting Jimmy's lack of physical coordination and his underdeveloped sense of cause and effect. Most likely, the glassware will break, Jimmy will be punished, but no positive lesson will have been learned."

Paul was 3 years old when he picked up his father's digital camera only to hear, "Paul, no! I'm warning you, this is not a toy. It's expensive. Put it down now!" Paul's natural curiosity presented a perfect opportunity for his father to teach the lesson of sharing rather than lecturing. At Paul's age he was certainly ready to intellectually participate in the concept of picture-taking and, more importantly, in a father-son exchange of sharing. The father's punishing explanation demeaned and showed disrespect for Paul. It sent the message that he was not old enough, trustworthy enough, or smart enough to hold the camera. It also says: I don't like sharing with you.

His father could have said, "Paul, would you like me to show you how the camera works?" or "Why don't you look at it, then I'll show you how it works." The message then would have been: Paul, I trust you. I like to share with you.

It should be emphasized that this philosophy of parenting does not advocate permissiveness. It advocates selectiveness and caring supervision. In other words, be in the process with your child—not intervening but interacting. This kind of generosity teaches the real meaning behind sharing.

Sharing will occur faster if an infant-turned-toddler has been given real freedom to explore, touch, and hold what he has identified as his.

4

A Different Way to Say "No"

WHICH STATEMENT WOULD elicit a more positive response from an adult when receiving bad news? "Sorry, you won't be going to the concert." Or, "Steve, I know you were looking forward to going to the concert, but the event is oversold and there were no tickets available. I know you're disappointed."

Although both statements carry the same bottom-line message, the latter is conveyed in a manner that shows you understand and feel the disappointment. The same communication principles that work so well with adults also work with children. They, too, will react more positively to a disappointing message if you carefully choose your words.

Many parents just use the word *no* to reject a request or stop a misbehavior. I prefer to think of the moment you are about to say "no" as the ideal time to teach self-discipline. This puts the parents' emphasis on the question How am I teaching my child inner self-control by the way in which I say "no"? What we really want in the long run is not for our children to listen to us, but to themselves—to hear their inner voice telling them right from wrong and to then act on that. That process must include an incentive for the toddler or child not to be rebellious, and that incentive is the freedom to express his feelings. If a child feels right, he will act right!

Toddlers are capable of far more self-restraint than we give them credit for. Given the proper cues, time, and respect, toddlers are quite capable of learning how to reason and choose the

Although it's true that often they do the opposite of what want, the point is they are quite capable of reasoning and making good choices. What they're lacking is precisely what you are trying to teach: coping skills and self-control.

As adults we know how difficult self-control can be to master. Knowing this can help you prevent an obstinate phase from becoming a pattern. Notice the way your 2-year-old looks at you the next time you ask him to do something for you. Sometimes you can see him wrestling with making a choice. Should I give the remote control back or run to the other end of the room with it? Should I keep using the Play-Doh or go downstairs and run around? These are early signs of your toddler learning decision-making and self-control. Parents should allow this individual process to develop before reprimanding or disciplining.

When someone asked Haim Ginott how many chances a parent should give a toddler, he replied, "A thousand chances, then give him one more." That really underscores the proper attitude and context in developing patience. However, parents have feelings and limits too! If a child pushes too far, it's the parent's turn to express his or her feelings. A parent may holler, "Todd, Daddy is angry that you put your crayons all over the wall! I'm very upset! Crayons belong on the paper. I'm furious with you." Controlled yelling allows the child to witness the natural expression of anger as it relates to a limit being broken. It also serves as a natural and healthy release for the parent. It's okay to let the child feel the emotional consequences of not having abided by what you'd asked. However, never degrade, humiliate, or compare him to anyone else when you express your anger. If you express disappointment through feelings, he will be far more encouraged to abide and listen to his conscience. After all, that's your primary goal—getting a toddler or child to ultimately govern himself in what is acceptable or unacceptable behavior. Over time a child will more easily accept this responsibility when he feels free to express his anger, disappointment, or frustration.

Paul's father was reading him a new book about trucks and kept asking his 3-year-old, "What's the name of this truck?" When Paul answered wrongly, his father repeatedly said, "No, it's called a flatbed truck." Paul will remember how many times he was wrong during that reading, and the word *no* will once again take a toll on his motivation and confidence. A better way to correct him would be to say, "Paul, try again. Let's try again." These simple words motivate; they don't debilitate.

It's easy to say "no" fast, especially when we're in a hurry. Many parents hear the repeated advice, "Don't be afraid to say the word *no*. It's okay to say it as many times as it takes." The truth is, rarely does the parent have to use the word *no* when turning down a request or stopping a misbehavior. Simply describing why something is unacceptable encourages the child to draw his own conclusions about why he can't do something or why he must stop. This principle of communication is a very powerful process that will help your child develop self-control more quickly. As many times as your child insists on something, that's how many times you give the facts or information. It's worth repeating here: It is not how fast you can get a child to stop, but how fast you can get him to think!

> Your primary goal is getting a toddler or child to ultimately govern himself in what is acceptable or unacceptable behavior. Over time a child will more easily accept this responsibility when he feels free to express his anger, disappointment, or frustration.

There are many ways to motivate a child to behave properly when having to tell him "no." Let's look at seven alternative expressions to use before we say "no" to encourage a child to control his inner impulses to act out. The following methods can be used interchangeably so as not to overuse or dilute the meaning of any singular idea. Showing a child this kind of patience and respect won't empower him—it will civilize him.

> Rarely does the parent have to use the word no when turning down a request or stopping a misbehavior. Simply describing why something is unacceptable encourages the child to draw his own conclusions about why he can't do something or why he must stop.

Before we examine alternative expressions as a substitute for saying "no," we must understand that these statements must be repeated about three or four times with an attitude of genuine empathy and respect. The goal is for the child to feel understood while the parent holds true to the limit he or she sets. In addition, outside of a few expressions, the process for saying "no" to a toddler is fundamentally the same for an older child. However, an older child has a much greater range to grasp the different meanings.

1. Acknowledge Their Feelings

"Andy, I see you're angry that your brother pushed you away. Use your words to tell Eric you don't like being pushed. Andy, I will not allow your brother to push you, the same way as I will not allow you to push your brother."

"Mary, I see you're sad that you have to leave the party."
"Alex, you're frustrated with that puzzle."
Principle: All feelings are allowed to be expressed.

2. Give Them a Choice

"Andy, you can have Cheerios or rice cakes. The choice is yours." "Eric, you can play with your puzzles or you can have clay. You make the choice."

"Samantha, you can put it back on the table or the chair. You decide."

Principle: You can reason and make choices.

3. When Possible, Substitute a "Yes" for a "No"

"Yes, Bobby, we can go to the park later." "Yes, Alan, you can go see your friend Mark later." "Yes, Cathy, we can have more candy later."

Principle: Show respect for the request and a willingness to do it.

4. When Possible, Demonstrate the Consequences

"Look, Bobby, there's no car in the driveway. There is no car to drive to the park." "Look, Matthew, see how sharp the scissors are." "Look, Cindy, feel how cold it is outside."

Principle: When possible, show concrete evidence why you are unable to do something.

5. Give Them in Fantasy What They Can't Have in Reality

"Bobby, you wish we could go swimming in a great big pool. It would be fun." "Mary, you wish Mommy could play with you now. You wish Mommy would stop everything now and just play with you. Mommy wishes it, too!" "Alex, you wish we had a great big bag of french fries now—with lots and lots of ketchup!

Daddy wishes it, too. I wish we could have 10 big bags of french fries now."

Principle: Granting a child his or her wishes shows empathy and respect. We all have wishes and fantasies. They are part of life.

6. Give the Information

"Sammy, Daddy has to mow the lawn first. I know you understand." "Nancy, Mommy would like to help but I must make a telephone call first. I know you understand."

"Alan, the car seat is in the other car. Mommy has only one car seat."

Principle: Allow the child to draw his or her own conclusions without being told "no."

7. Give Yourself Time to Reflect

"Samantha, I would like to think about that." "Sally, that's a good idea. I want to think about it today." "Megan, I want to talk about it tonight with Dad. I want to consider it."

Principle: Show the child respect—that you will consider his or her request instead of instantly saying "no." This also teaches the child about hope and disappointment.

Careful, Words Are Like Bullets!

ALTHOUGH PARENTS' actions remain the final example for toddlers and children to follow, a parent must first choose the right words. It's astonishing to notice the casual and colloquial vocabulary that adults sometimes use in front of their children. Somehow words have lost their meaning and value. I've always wished that words would come with warning labels the way medications do. **Caution: These words may produce side effects.**

A child may hear, "Billy, your room is a mess. You live like a pig," or "Marilyn, you're being a bad girl, sit still in your chair." Today, it seems that family dialogue reflects the relaxed social norm of "it's okay to say anything." Thinking no longer appears to be a prerequisite; all that matters is self-expression! People don't look for the right words—they say, "Forget what I say, you know what I mean," or "Bobby is acting silly; let's ignore him." I submit that a large part of the out-of-control behavior that is exhibited between children and their families is due to the parents' lack of thought about the words they use. A child's acting out becomes more explosive with each word that discounts their sense of self. A parent may scold, "Bobby, you're acting and crying like your baby brother," or "Linda, if you continue to act silly you're going to get a time-out!"

> A large part of the out-of-control behavior that is exhibited between children and their families is due to the parents' lack of thought about the words they use.

A better response for encouraging cooperation is to acknowledge behavior through description rather than personal attacks: "Bobby, Mommy can see that you're upset and you don't want to go," or "Linda, it's hard to sit still and wait. I see you're having a difficult time waiting!" Sometimes the right words are more important than the right actions. However, these are not magic words. If children continually see their parents lose their tempers, have been made to feel inadequate through comparisons ("Tommy, your sister would never act the way you do") or harsh name calling ("Nancy, quit acting stupid"), or hear a constant stream of threats ("Bobby, if you do that again, Mommy is going to put you in your room for a time-out"), they will not want to stop their misbehaviors. The right words function as guideposts for helping children focus on learning self-control. Respecting children won't empower them to act out; it will civilize them to act right!

The most common well-meaning parental response to children's expressions of how they feel is what I call the "no, you're not" rule. When you say to a child, "No, you're not tired," or "No, that's not nice to say," or "No, you didn't mean that," you're saying your child's feelings not only don't count, but worse, are wrong in what they sense to be true. How can we expect our children to grow up trusting themselves if we teach them what they feel is not real?

A more effective approach would be to reflect the mood of the situation. For example, you could say, "I know you're tired"; "I see how angry you are at Tommy"; or "Sounds like you don't like your teacher." Parents who deny children's feelings systematically teach them not to trust their own feelings and instincts. By doing so, parents suggest that their child should rely instead on the parent's feelings and perceptions. In adolescence and adulthood, such behavior is manifested with frequent expressions of "I don't know how I feel; I'm confused." When these children become adults, their insecurity and lack of identity will often lead them to seek the approval and opinions of others. They easily identify with how the other person feels about what they are telling them. It's as though they are asking, "Because I am confused, will you tell me how I should feel?" That's why if children always feel free to express their feelings, they will have more confidence as they get older to trust their own instincts and feelings when they have to make key life decisions.

As adults we sometimes find ourselves apologizing to each other and taking words back. Our maturity allows for that process and growth to take place. However, the same maturity is not present in children. Words cannot be taken back. As Ginott says, "Words are like bullets." They can pierce the inner spirit. Children may forgive but they don't forget!

It is more effective to describe the actions you want a child to adopt rather than to attack her character or personality. "Marilyn, when we're in the restaurant, I'm expecting you to stay seated. I know it can be difficult."

Thinking about the right words sets the backdrop for the right attitude. This change in attitude will help bring a more calm and relaxed reaction from you the next time you have to refuse a demand from your toddler or child. Words are critical—choose them thoughtfully. Remember, building respect is cumulative. Naturally, toddlers will act out to test their powers as well as the parents' consistency in maintaining the limit. The secret is how you respond to your child's transgression. Be patient and consistent with your respect and, sooner rather than later, he will begin to abide by your requests. Children may not always obey, but they almost always listen. In other words, they *do* hear you, but they don't want to abide!

Alternatives to Saying "No"

CONSIDER AN interim expression that will allow your toddler or child to feel better about herself when you have to deny a request or correct a misbehavior. The phrase "I know you understand" can be said after you have clearly explained a misbehavior and you know she understands. How you say something can be as important as what you say. Your tone should be positive, not foreboding. Your words should convey a confidence that you have in your child. Say this new expression to yourself ("I know you understand") and feel the difference in yourself when compared to a common put-down response of "No, don't do that!" The right choice of words, along with an understanding but firm tone, will encourage the right behavior and the right feelings in both you and your child.

Why These Words Work

The phrase "I know you understand" teaches four lessons:

1. You are expressing respect for your child because you are telling him you know that he knows better.
2. It allows him to think about his misbehavior without the fear of punishment. This will help develop his conscience.
3. You're telling him he has the intelligence to understand.
4. You have the confidence in him to correct the misbehavior.

One father might reprimand his 4-year-old, "Don't you understand what I'm talking about? Am I going to have to tell you again?" Another father might say, "Alex, I know you understand." What a difference the right words can make! "I know you understand" conveys all the right messages: You're smart, I trust you, I respect you. The right words help teach self-mastery and self-worth. Use these teachable moments to motivate your child to do the right thing. Over time, he will do it more and more!

Five Reasons Why Giving Facts Works Better Than Saying the Word *No*

1. Allows the child to reason and come to his own answers and conclusions

2. Takes the focus away from the perception and feeling that the parent is being unfair and heavy-handed

3. Does not make the parent the messenger of the word *no*

4. Shows respect for the child's ability to understand

5. Reduces feelings of resentment from the child

Summary

WHAT SHOULD parents do when their child misbehaves and they have to say "no"? The answer lies again in using the right words. Sometimes it's more what you say than what you do. Many parents think managing their toddler's tantrum requires an immediate action. That's understandable because it's hard to listen and watch screaming and disruptiveness. However, before carrying her away, pulling her back, or lifting her up, you should leave her with the right words. A toddler or child hearing "I know you know better. Dirt from the floor doesn't belong on your sandwich. I know you understand," rather than "Didn't I tell you before, don't you listen . . ." will make her want to abide faster. This will strengthen her self-control and help her calm down faster.

The secret to bringing out the best in your child is to bring out the best in yourself!

5

Why Don't
Kids Listen?

WHAT DO WE really mean when we ask, "Are you listening?" The act of listening has, after all, two meanings. First, it can mean to hear and gather information or; it can also mean to follow instruction. This is an important distinction. Although children may often choose to tune out and not abide, you can be sure they heard what you said! So when a parent says, "Paul, what's the matter with you, didn't you hear me?" Paul thinks, "Nothing's the matter with me, I *did* hear you! I just don't want to do what you ask." Paul will also feel put down by the implied sarcasm, as it insults his intelligence and attentiveness. *Children may not always obey but they almost always listen.*

Most children who do *not* listen (abide) are simply shutting down. The feeling of "here comes another lecture" or "my feelings will probably be ignored anyway" will bring this on. It's ironic that as adults we labor for so long and practice so hard to achieve good listening skills, yet so early in our child's life we insist they perfect what has been so difficult for us to do as adults. It helps to not attach unrealistic expectations to our children's behavior, thinking, "Next time my child will listen better."

The truth is, children forget and need to be reminded again and again to think and listen. The secret to accelerating that process lies in *how* we remind them. Better to say, "Tommy, what can I do to help you remember?" than, "What's the matter with you; you always forget?"

What is it about this fundamental skill that is so difficult? More importantly, *why* is this fundamental skill so resisted? How can we expect our children by the time they are 3, 4, 7, or 8 to listen to us if they feel *we* have not listened to *them?* If we want our children to comply faster, we must be aware of the huge role this fact plays. Listening involves not only the physical discipline of *alertness* but, more importantly, requires an *authentic* interest (and response) in what is being said. Children, just as adults, know when a person is listening sincerely, contrasted with that person just waiting for the opportunity to interrupt and talk again. Too often children are interrupted before being able to finished their complete thoughts. Leading child psychologist and play therapist Garry Landreth, in his new book with Arthur Kraft, *Parents As Therapeutic Partners—Listening to Your Child's Play*, emphasizes the critical importance of parents slowing down their communication and imparting the feeling of complete attentiveness. This process, though it sounds easy, requires enormous focus and patience. Children need time to formulate their ideas and need to know a parent won't abandon their feelings and ideas haphazardly. Can you imagine being in a business meeting and having your boss cut you off because it was taking you too long to express an idea or because you tried to reframe it another way? The truth is, I'll bet you can.

How Can I Show My 4-Year-Old I Am Listening?

WHEN 4-YEAR-OLD Allan tells his mother he is afraid of the dog on the street, she may unwittingly say, "Allan, it is only a small dog, there is nothing to be afraid of, he doesn't bite. You're a big boy now, it's okay." For Allan, hearing these words confirms his feelings that Mommy didn't *listen* and doesn't understand. As if that isn't enough, Allan is also made to feel ashamed by having his courage judged. After all, big boys shouldn't be afraid. A more effective response from his mother would have been, "Yes, Allan, dogs can be scary. When you don't know an animal you might think, 'Hmm, I wonder what this dog is like?' Sometimes just thinking about different dogs can be scary. Some are big and some are small. Some are friendly and some are not. I'm glad you told me."

Similarly, if Allan's mother explained to her husband she was afraid to fly on an airplane because of all the unfortunate airline tragedies she had read about and was told, "Honey, there is nothing to be afraid of; what you saw on television is a different airline going to a different destination. It's okay, you'll be safe," these words understandably would do little to alleviate her anxiety. Here, the husband could have said, "Honey, with all the tragedies, I can understand why you would be afraid. It makes sense." Adults—just like children—do *not* want to be talked out of their feelings. They want to feel supported so they can conquer their own anxieties by saying, in effect, to themselves, "Hey, I did good. I got through it."

Award-winning author and lecturer John Bradshaw, who I consider to be a towering force in helping people come to terms with painful early childhood experiences, has focused primarily on those individuals who suffered traumatically at the hands of their parents or primary caretakers. However, his powerful message—to recognize *once and for all* the enormous capacity of a young infant or child to feel shame and embarrassment at so early an age—is now widely recognized.

As Ginott repeatedly and so eloquently put it, *"Treat your child as though he is the person he is already capable of becoming."* In order for these generational patterns to stop, parents must make extra efforts to evaluate themselves in relation to how and what they communicate to their children.

Take More Time

IT IS easy to understand why many parents do not listen to their children when they voice their resistance to what is being asked of them. From a practical point of view, *really* listening to a child and looking behind the behavior takes concentrated time. It also probably won't get the child to abide right away anyway. Parents who are in a hurry and have to be somewhere fast hardly have the time to go through this process. The fastest way to achieve this is to intimidate, bully, threaten, or just whisk the child away without explanation. Even some contemporary psychologists insist we should say, "Just do it because I say so."

However, if a parent can step back and allow a more human process to take place and reflect the mood and expectation of the child, then the long-term cumulative effects will take shape and the foundation for mutual respect and cooperation will have been set. This foundation of feeling understood is why children, all on their own, comply faster. *If a child feels right, he will act right!*

Listening can take many forms. We are always telling our children to listen with ears but *we* sometimes forget to *listen with our eyes.* When 18-month-old Darren would not leave a friend's house when his mother said, "It's time to go, Darren," she quickly turned her pleasant tone into a mean *threat.* "Darren, Mommy's leaving without you." Although Darren quickly dropped what he was doing and rushed toward the door, his mom didn't *listen* to the expression on his face, which was panic and fear. Instead she was proud of how quickly she got her son to abide. For a toddler or any young child, being told that a mother or father will leave them behind is a devastating message. *All* children carry within them a natural fear of abandonment; when a parent threatens to leave somewhere without them, they are making their child's fear real.

So real, it becomes their worst nightmare come true.

Looking at Ourselves As Parents

THE SOCIAL pressures of bringing children up so that they appear to have all the advantages results in the average parent wanting to appear to friends and family as if he or she has it "all together." Although it's not popular to say so, good parenting is *not* intuitive. It is a learned skill. When some adults first hear this, they may react defensively as if this were an attack on their intelligence and commitment as parents. For those of you who believe good parenting *is* intuitive, just ask yourself two questions: How many times a day are you unsure about how you discipline your child? Parents need *not* be embarrassed in recognizing that healthy, effective communication is learned. It is a well-known secret among professionals who work with children that part of the problem is how to tell the parents or parent about what they may be doing in such a way so as not to threaten their image of themselves as good moms or dads. The typical concern for the professional is, "If I don't tell a parent in just the right way they will likely become defensive, not listen, and withdraw from the process!" Just as our body signals an alarm when we feel pain, our conscience signals our heart when it is in pain. An ancient saying makes this point: *"The superior man will watch over himself when he is alone. He examines his heart that there may be nothing wrong there, and that he may have no cause of dissatisfaction with himself."*

There is no greater favor you can do for your child than to acknowledge and accept his or her feelings. This doesn't mean you accept all behavior, just all feelings. Over time, this will translate directly to your child listening more and responding faster to your requests. In the name of love, parents sometimes teach lessons of self-control to their children through screaming, nagging, name calling, sarcasm, threats, and sometimes even hitting. Later, when the parents feel bad, they say, "I do these things because I love you." Love is what *parents* say they need to give. However, from a child's viewpoint, understanding and respect is what *children* need to get. Getting this message through to parents is more difficult than getting children to listen. (I am convinced that parents who are totally committed to loving their children believe that whatever unwitting careless acts of discipline that cause their child pain will be forgotten years later anyway!) A quote from Oscar Wilde comes to mind: *"In the beginning children love their parents, after a while they judge them, rarely if ever do they forgive them."* If this seems rather harsh sounding, it is said only to help us stay honest with ourselves.

The social pressures of bringing children up so that they appear to have all the advantages results in the average parent wanting to appear to friends and family as if he or she has it "all together."

6

Setting Limits

ALL PARENTS AGREE that children need limits. What they don't agree on are the methods and the timing for setting them. They live with their children from moment to moment, exacting obedience or excusing disobedience on whim rather than on principle.

The solution to this predicament, however, may lie in the approach. Some parents think that setting limits is a one-time event. It shouldn't be. It is a dynamic process that keeps changing. What you say "no" to in the morning may become "yes" at lunchtime. For example, a mother may mistakenly say to her 3-year-old, "Ellen, no more juice *today!*" A contradiction arises if the child gets juice in the afternoon. What is required here is a casual but firm attitude in providing the correct information or instruction. "Ellen, you had three glasses this morning. I know you wish you could have more, but we're finished for this morning."

Young children respond better to limits when parents are specific rather than general in what they *will* or *will not* allow. For example, if a parent says, "Tommy, you can only bang *a little* on the chair," Tommy will see this as an invitation to test his limit. Does "little" mean three times, ten times, or fifteen times? He will make sure he finds out! Better to say, "Tommy, you can bang the chair two times." Although he will probably still bang the chair a third time, he will *not* be confused about what the limit was at the time of his consequence. The consequence will also not be perceived as a trick or a surprise—unpopular yes, but not unfair. Children respond better to limit setting when parents provide concrete, rather than abstract, information. Five-year-old Nathan will respond better to "It's time to leave in 5 minutes" rather than "Soon it is time to leave."

Sometimes parents will prepare a child to believe that they "mean business" by faking a stern look, threatening a consequence, or lowering their voice with seriousness. They believe this will have a greater impact on their child. It doesn't. Children can read and gauge how authentic and committed parents are. However, when used correctly, voice, hands, facial expressions, and actions become the *real* tools for keeping potential problems from escalating. Consistency in setting and handling limits on the part of the parent will determine how easily new limits will be accepted.

Child psychologist Louise Guerney says that, as a rule, limits should be set in relation to what is *really* important to you and your child. They should be enforced "*every single time* they are broken." This is key if a child is to really believe you mean what you say. In addition to the psychological benefits derived from it, setting limits allows a child to both *feel* safe and *be* safe. As a result, enforcement of your promised limit also helps the child to be less anxious and less empowered. Conversely, unenforced limits will cause increased anxiety in your child's everyday life with you as a result of not knowing when or how your hammer of discipline will fall. The child will think, "I know I broke the rule," and become anxious about when the punishment or retaliation will occur. In addition to this anxiety, he becomes more empowered from the parents' inability to correct his misbehavior. Parents who are not skillful in maintaining limits bestow a certain authority to the child. This could lead to the child to think, "I'm smarter and tougher than you." It is confirmation for him that he has defeated an adult. Although he celebrates his victory, he is also scared and uncertain of his new power. Who will keep him safe? Who will protect him? That is why a parent must think twice before setting a limit or rule about a particular behavior. Parents must ask themselves, "Is this limit necessary? Does it fit the situation? Can it be enforced?"

A limit or a rule that is heavy-handed and not fair is sometimes worse than no limit at all. For example, 4-year-old Carol was touching the packages of candy while waiting in line at the supermarket with her mother. "Carol, *no!* Stand still and do not move while we are in line!" Yet, a few moments later, the line started to move. When Carol didn't move, her mother grabbed her arm, pulled her, and yelled, "Carol, move! Why are you standing still?" Carol was probably thinking, "You told me not to move."

Alex was 3 1/2 years old. One afternoon his mother took him in the car to run errands with her. She told him, "Alex, I'm warning you, if you don't behave, I'm going to take you home." This simple statement had three problems with it. First, the mother had no intention of stopping her errands, so there could be no en-

> A parent must think twice before setting a limit or rule about a particular behavior. Parents must ask themselves, "Is this limit necessary? Does it fit the situation? Can it be enforced?"

forcement of the limit. Second, the limit "behave" was so general that it gave Alex no room to be himself. What does it mean to *behave?* Children need specific information: "Alex, I am expecting you to *not* run through the stores at the mall when we get there. I know you understand." Third, the earlier threat Alex received ("Alex, I'm warning you") served as a message that said, I expect you to misbehave. Unfortunately, this type of communication creates a challenge and ultimately a power struggle.

The secret in dealing with misbehaviors lies in the combination of not making it a contest between the parent and child and the patience for dealing with a transgression. Although your child may test your limit three, four, or five times, your mood, calming style (or angry response, when called for), and promised consequence should remain consistent. This way when you're ready to set the next limit, it will become easier for both you and your child. When rules, reactions, and consequences are predictable, less energy is required to communicate them.

Some parents have difficulty in setting and maintaining any limits on their child's behavior (except in the face of dangerous situations) for fear of being rejected. Their own need to be loved may make it too painful to risk having their child say hurtful things to them. When 4-year-old Melanie won't leave the playground after four or five requests, the strongest response her mother can muster is, "Please, Melanie, please; you're not being fair." This type of ineffective communication sets no real limits for the child and won't provide the results the parent is seeking.

At the other extreme are those parents who put too heavy a restriction or too many limits on their child's behavior both at home and on the outside. The danger in setting too many limits is that such limits will ultimately cause the child to fight and rebel against your limits, ignore them, or find ways to cheat to get around them.

Try to handle setting limits in a positive way, as the family in the following example did. Before getting ready to sit down for dinner, everyone in the family always washes their hands in the kitchen sink. Today 5-year-old Nancy didn't.

MOM: "Nancy, do you remember the rule about washing your hands before dinner?"

NANCY: "No, I don't."

MOTHER: "Nancy, what can I do to help you remember? You know the rule is no eating dinner together until your hands are washed."

NANCY: "I don't want to."

MOTHER: "Well, I understand you don't want to wash your hands. However, you know the rule. If you want to have dinner at the table you must wash your hands first. Nancy, you decide what to do."

If Nancy still insists on not eating, respect her choice. Do *not* extend the consequences beyond the dinner hour. If later she wants a snack, that's okay. There is no need to admonish or remind her about her earlier choice. From a child's point of view, lectures and long explanations are a signal of weakness in a parent's willpower. Children interpret these long talks as "my parents would rather talk than act."

The consequences for a transgression must always be balanced with the degree of seriousness for that transgression. For example, toddlers' obnoxious behaviors such as whining ("Pick me up, pick me up!" or "More, more, more!") are really more annoying than deserving of punishment. Parents need to calmly allow this process to play out, which will reinforce the message, "I am not going to change my mind, so you need to change your behavior." You may say, for example, "Betsy, I see you want more. I wish you could have more, but I told you, only one. You can play here and have fun or you can play in your room. The choice is yours. I see you're angry. I wish you could have more. But you can't. You make the choice. Play here or in your room."

How you talk to your child in one stage of development will be remembered in the next. The principles, as well as the philosophy that supports these behavioral strides, are based on repetition and patience. A good example to illustrate this is 3-year-old

> How you talk to your child in one stage of development will be remembered in the next. The principles, as well as the philosophy that supports these behavioral strides, are based on repetition and patience.

Matthew, who was having a difficult time being potty trained. Although his parents extolled what a big boy he was when he remembered to use his potty, they treated him like a baby at home or in public with constant restrictions placed upon him. "Matthew, *no*. Don't go near that. You're not old enough!" or "Matthew, those toys are for babies. Here . . . play with this instead." Matthew was trying to outgrow one stage of development (potty training) and feel a different kind of self-sufficiency. However, he was constantly reminded by his mother or father that somehow he was still a baby and not old enough to be trusted. Parents should try to maintain consistency in matching the right words with each stage to help bring about children's natural maturity.

These new methods of communicating with your child are not intended to work immediately. What will work immediately is starting the child's process of focusing on his own behavior and need for self-control, rather than focusing on the conflict between his parent and himself. That is why a toddler or child should be given so many chances to make the right decision on his own. Over time, the focus remains on his behavior, not the parent's control.

Allow Your Child to Complain

A KEY element in setting and maintaining limits is *not* to set a time limit on how long you allow your toddler or child to complain. "Bobby, quit crying already! Act like a big boy! I'm going to ignore you if you keep complaining! If you keep it up we're not going!" Naturally, it is upsetting and frustrating for a parent to listen to such carrying on. Each parent, just as each child, has a different tolerance level for frustration and disappointment. However, allowing toddlers or children to cry, whine, or complain for as long as they like, without criticizing or demeaning them, will diminish the length of their tantrum or outburst.

During this process, the parent should continually reflect (mirror) the child's feelings, disappointment, and fantasies about their state of mind. If parents reflect their child's state of mind in a sort of natural sincere soliloquy, then their bad mood or temper will likely diminish significantly. For example, you might say, "Alex, I know you're mad that we have to go now; I know you're angry at Daddy for taking you away from your toys. It's time to go but we will be back." (Pause) "Everything will be here waiting for you when we come back. I know you want to stay. I see you're angry. We will come back and visit." In the beginning, this may go on for two, five, or ten minutes. Alex (although he can't express it yet) will remember the way you understood his frustration and

anger rather than the enforcement of the limit. If you do not empathize with his feelings, he will internalize a repressed inner
anger that may erupt at a later time, at which point the parent
would say, "I don't understand, it came from nowhere!" *When
children feel right, they act right!*

Ironically, the child's repressed anger would not have been
over the disappointment of having been told "no," but rather
from his feelings of being dismissed and ignored. When you narrate or mirror a child's feelings, the intensity of his outburst is
lessened. This is because he feels satisfied in knowing he is at the
center of your attention and is understood. During this process,
your attitude when reflecting a child's feelings must be sincere
and authentic. Children know when something is said gratu-
itously and falsely. Insincerity will just further enrage them.

It's really no different for adults. You have probably witnessed
a store closing just shortly before someone arrives. When the
storekeeper says, "I'm sorry, no, I can't let you in," the customer
does a little "speech dance" to persuade the person to open the
store. When this doesn't work, the customer goes further, creating
some concocted story about an emergency or saying, "I'll be real
quick." After these exchanges, you can see the customer becoming more frustrated and angry and unable to accept a flat "no."
This may lead to a ranting and raving about how the person will
never shop at this store again and how he or she will tell friends
never to shop here, either. Had the storekeeper *acknowledged* and
accepted the customer's frustration and anger, the customer would
have felt understood and would have maturely accepted the store
being closed: "I'm sorry. I see how angry you are. I'm sure you
drove a long way. I wish I could re-open. Our policy is all doors
close at 6 P.M. I understand how disappointed you are." Think

how much better you would feel being talked to this way. Why is it any different for a toddler or child?

In addition, it is important that when a limit is set and the child does transgress that the parent reflect an attitude that still conveys *I know you knew better.* Convey confidence in your child. The emphasis should be on both the attitude of the correction and a confidence that you know next time he or she will do better. Sometimes just a look or a word can say volumes more than little speeches and can help the child focus on his own behavior. Parents should understand that not all misbehaviors need to be commented on. Trusting a child to know when he has transgressed aids the child in developing his sense of right and wrong and is at the core of what we want the toddler or child to learn.

> It is important that when a limit is set and the child does transgress that the parent reflect an attitude that still conveys *I know you knew better.* Convey confidence in your child.

Of course, consequences must be consistent with what a parent said they would be. Therefore, when a child or toddler tries to push through his or her limits, a parent must still hold to his or hers.

Provide the Right Message

A CHILD'S maturity level is key to his understanding of what you're saying "no" to. If he has not sufficiently matured, then your command has no meaning and will only spark confusion and frustration. Saying "no" is not a one-dimensional action—it's not just saying, "No, Bobby," and then Bobby stops and that's that. There are three stages a child goes through when responding to the word *no*. The child feels its impact emotionally, tries to understand it intellectually, and needs to cope with the disappointment. In the beginning, it may take up to 10 minutes to say "no" properly.

The next time you find yourself having to reject what your child is doing, watch your child's face during and after you explain a misbehavior. Let him sense your sincere desire to understand his disappointment. This is a good time to emotionally connect with how he is feeling. This doesn't mean you need to beg for his permission or plead for his acceptance when saying "no." It is, however, the right time to reflect how he is feeling. If he is unable to verbalize his feelings at this time, use this as an opportunity to get in tune with him. One way is to reflect or mirror his mood. "Andy, I see how frustrated and angry you are that we have to leave now." This kind of communication builds trust, not resentment. It is based on the fundamental principle of showing respect for a child's feelings without weakening or changing the limit that was set by the parent. The child may still throw a tantrum from knowing he will not get his way, but that is very different from a tantrum centered in feeling dismissed. The result of this consistent style of communicating will more quickly bring about self-control for your child and harmony within the family.

Respected leadership lecturer and author Stephen Covey talks about his concept of building harmony through creating "goodwill." He says that goodwill is like a bank account. Adults draw on it within their relationships. It is an underlying attitude that conveys, "You are a worthy person." You can use the same principle with children. I call it the "trust account," and it requires big deposits. It begins by conferring responsibility without threat of consequences or rebuke. For example, if a father and son are working in the garage, the father may say, "Here, Bobby, hold the hammer for Daddy. Later we can put the nails in the wood together." Many times parents will begin to talk correctly to their child in this manner and then become frustrated and angry when the child takes advantage of the situation. The child is banging too soon! We should always be prepared for this to happen. Part of a child's daily job (if he or she is to grow in a healthy way) is to challenge him- or herself and the world. Learning is a cumulative and integrated process.

Among many other parenting objectives, our daily job is to help our children strengthen their own self-control. We do this by saying (when things get out of control), "Bobby, I see you're having difficulty putting the hammer down," or "Sometimes it's hard for you to control yourself." Though the end result will probably be physically taking the hammer away from Bobby, there won't be any attack on his character or personality. Bobby will still feel deserving of the trust you showed him. In return and after months of this type of communication, he will begin trusting you more by openly showing his feelings and abiding by your requests.

> If we recognize that our children have the same intensities of feelings we do and we allow that discharge to take place, we are making way for new behavior and new productivity.

If we recognize that our children have the same intensities of feelings we do and we allow that discharge to take place, we are making way for new behavior and new productivity. If this sounds a little like therapy, it is. The difference is you won't have to send your child for weekly visits and you save the $500 a month!

The consistency and respect you show for your child's ability to understand what you are saying will have a profound impact on your relationship now and into adolescence. If you are already doing this, then your "trust account" is getting bigger and your relationship is getting better!

Consequences

THERE ARE three basic consequences that can occur when a child does not abide. The first consequence is the punishment for the transgression, such as a time-out, a certain look, or maybe not going somewhere your child wanted to go. The importance of *not* talking about the punishment before the transgression occurs should be noted here. Talking about it beforehand undermines a child's confidence to do the right thing in the first place. A threat of consequences serves as a challenge to her autonomy. A parent may say, "Linda, we have to go in 5 minutes. If you don't leave in 5 minutes, I'm not taking you to the movies." This type of threat and communication puts the focus on the conflict and creates a challenge. And a challenge, in all likelihood, will become a fight.

In contrast, a parent's promise of a future punishment or consequence that comes *after* a child's repeated transgressions and refusal to listen will not be perceived as heavy-handed. Because the parent gave the child both the proper warning to stop and enough time to self-correct, the child understands more clearly that the consequence is a result of her own misbehavior and not a random act of control by the parent. For best results, refer to the principles in the 7-Step Method in chapter 8, which avoids threats altogether. In the long run, this allows the child to come to her own conclusions, which in turn builds self-regulation.

The second—and maybe even more important—lesson of telling a child why she should not do something are the possible *physical* consequences of the act. For example, what happens if she drops the glass on the floor? What happens if he puts chocolate on the walls or touches a hot cup of coffee? Without the parent thoughtfully explaining the reasons behind why they will not allow a certain behavior (and demonstrating when possible), the child is left to his or her own imagination. Calm, patient, and straightforward information goes a long way in helping the child accept the parent's position. Extra effort and attention for this set of consequences will often help to prevent future accidents. Even if the child doesn't abide, it is ultimately the parent's behavior that reinforces the right behavior for learning self-control. "Alice, if the glass breaks on the floor, the sharp edges could cut our feet," or "Chocolate is for eating. I get angry when chocolate is put on the walls."

The third and final consequence of turning your child down the wrong way are the emotional feelings your child is left with. Today, the popular opinions of some experts boast, "Parents waste too much time focusing on a child's feelings." These professionals believe in the adage "Do it because I say so." Parents who lack patience agree. The result is often random outbursts from the parents trying everything from reasoning to spanking to quiet down their child. In the end, neither the parent nor the child ever knows what the other will really do during a conflict. Every thing is moment to moment. Borne from these frustrations comes the final technique of angrily "willing your way over theirs." In the end, these techniques are all self-defeating. Some experts say fear of rejection from our children combined with not wanting to do them psychological harm have rendered parents weak and powerless.

What we really need, these experts continue to say, is a return to the old philosophy of, "I'm the parent. I said so, that's it!" The results, they say, are that good behavior is maximized and discussions and debates are minimized. I believe intimidation or heavy-handed parenting is a recipe for both short- and long-term resentment on the part of both parent and child. It's true that intimidation and fear *will* work in the short run. The problem is in the long run a child will often secretly plan his revenge. During the 1950s, these were also common motivating factors in our classrooms. Back then, the baseline IQ of a child was the yardstick for achievement. For children whose IQ was average or better than average, fear and intimidation did little to affect performance. Those children fundamentally coped and performed well. But if a child's IQ wasn't at least average or he was having emotional difficulties, then he gave up on himself right then and there! A child who is pushed too hard would rather appear that he *won't* do something rather than face the truth that he *can't* do something. This enormous waste of human potential can be felt for generations.

We have since learned that without the right kind of encouragement ("Mary, let's look it another way," or "Tommy, let's try again together"), a child's motivation to achieve his potential can be discharged almost entirely. Those flawed hard-line approaches that demean the human spirit fail both in the school system and the family system. In his book *How Children Fail*, educator John Holt may have best described intelligence by saying, "It is not how much we know how to do, but how we *behave* when we don't know what to do!"

The potential of each individual to fulfill their destiny is ultimately steeped in his or her own belief in themselves. But where does this belief come from? Although there are exceptions, this "I can do it" attitude comes from the influence of at least one other person. That is why I believe the goal is not to see how *fast* you can get a child to stop a misbehavior, but how *long* you give that child a chance to *do right.* Children need endless chances, information, and explanations to develop the right moral compass and inner self-control. Again, this might sound like a license for permissiveness, but when consistently communicated, these principles will win over even the most ornery child. It is again worth repeating: *If a child feels right, he will act right.*

A deeper and more extended meaning of this process can be likened to watching a foreign film without subtitles. Without the words, you only understand half the picture! It is the same for your child. He can only understand the world through your narration and explanation. "Brian, you see that little girl crying over there? She's crying because her mom took those cookies away from her." This helps Brian understand why she is crying so that he won't feel anxious that maybe he'll be next.

Sometimes children feel things that seem totally unrelated to the present moment. For Brian, watching that exchange between the mom and the little girl may remind him of something that occurred at an earlier time at home or maybe on television. As a result of the kind of communication used by Brian's mom, a toddler or child can now make sense of himself in relation to his family and the outside world. Children count on us to narrate facts and categorize emotions. Sometimes an interpretation of a situation is necessary: "Bobby, that little boy is frustrated that he can't put his shoe on," or "Tammy, look—the cat is scared!"

Without your input, your child will either guess the answers to his questions or, worse, other people with different answers, styles, and perhaps values will teach their own point of view. This is why so many professionals regard the parent as the child's first real and final teacher.

Toddlers Know When They Misbehave

WHEN SAMMY, a 3-year-old, is throwing his toys, or 2-year-old Lilly is spilling her food on the floor, you invariably hear the parent say, "No, don't throw it on the floor." The question here is, Do you think the toddler didn't know that? Outside of a few misbehaviors, most toddlers and children know when they misbehave. Telling them "no" repeatedly sends the message, "You're not smart, so I have to keep reminding you!"

Describing behavior works better: "Looks like you're finished playing with your Legos," or "You must be finished with your food because you're throwing it on the floor." You can also tell the child, "I know you know better." This sends the message that you have confidence in him or her to stop.

Relentless reprimands reinforce infantile behavior and build no self-confidence or trust between the parent and child. The need for more than one reprimand also means that the parent probably did not enforce the limit that was set. Parents must not only remain consistent in enforcing that limit, but they must also allow their child to emotionally act out no matter how obnoxious his behavior. The trick is in allowing your child to expend his own energy while you remain firm but calm, all the while reflecting his mood and disappointment. Although this may take five, ten, or even fifteen minutes, sooner rather than later your child will begin to say to himself, "I will find another way."

It's no secret that toddlers and children will forever push and pull to get their way as they pass through these formative years. Remember, part of the child's daily routine is to look for ways to make the parent act out. *It's important that all children push their limits from time to time.* This behavior develops individual fortitude and confidence and is only one of the ways they test their own limits and the parent's will and consistency. Unfortunately, most times children are successful in expanding their limits. However, the parent must still strive to maintain and enforce the limit imposed.

> It's important that all children push their limits from time to time. This behavior develops individual fortitude and confidence and is only one of the ways they test their own limits and the parent's will and consistency.

Threats

WHAT DO most "no's" and threats have in common? Simply this: They ignore what a child was thinking and feeling while she was being told "no." Parents are sometimes so eager to stop their child's actions that they stop their feelings in the process. As Haim Ginott once said, "Certain patterns of relating to children are almost always self-defeating."

A constant stream of threats is one of the patterns that contributes to a child's misbehavior. Ginott states, "To children, threats are invitations to repeat a forbidden act. When a child is told, 'If you do it once more . . .' he does not hear the words 'if you.' He hears only 'do it once more.' Sometimes he interprets it as 'Mother expects me to do it once more, or she'll be disappointed.' Such warnings, fair as they may seem to adults, are worse than useless. They make sure that an obnoxious act will be repeated. A warning serves as a challenge to the child's autonomy. If he has any self-respect he must transgress again to show himself and others he is not afraid."

Bribes

BRIBERY ELICITS an entirely different response from a child. When Katie's mom told her, "No, you can't go outside and play," Katie began to throw her usual tantrum. Her mom thought she cleverly outwitted Katie by bribing her with her favorite candy if she would stay inside and "be good." Though this seemed to work for a while, Katie was developing her own interpretation of these events. Katie was learning to be bad and felt almost an obligation to maintain her "badness" so she could continue to get her candy. In turn she felt her mom was getting her money's worth (her goodness). However, Katie also developed a feeling of guilt when she received the candy from her mom at other times when she wasn't bad.

Here, the guilt was felt because she didn't feel she had *earned* the candy. After all, she wasn't being bad. So naturally and for no reason apparent to her mother, Katie began to misbehave every time her mother gave her candy, no matter what the circumstances. These patterns become clearer over time, and the blackmail or payoff became increasingly higher for the promised good behavior. Although some parents regard this behavior as "cute negotiating," in reality it prevents a child from learning how to control her impulses and instead reinforces manipulation, dishonesty, and resentment.

How to Say "No" in a Toy Store

HOW MANY times have we walked past a toy store in the mall or driven by one in the car and had our kids call out, cry, or beg for a new toy—"Please Dad, please"? Sometimes we can inadvertently create this expectation when we communicate in a way that is not clear or that sets a different expectation for our children. "Okay, Linda, let's go to the toy store." Over time, hearing the word *go* somehow raises greater expectations than the word *visit*. This can be one of the most misunderstood and missed opportunities to teach your toddler that the world is not on display for her to own but to visit and share. Although this may sound unrealistic, your children *will* change their reactions over time if they are given a different expectation. Beginning at about 20 months, toddlers are able to begin to accept that *wanting* does not always mean *getting*.

Don't Just Go . . . Visit

We teach that we *visit* friends but don't take home their toys; we *visit* parks and don't take home the playground equipment. So why can't we *visit* stores without having to buy something? We can! The key is to prepare the expectation before leaving the house. A toy store can be a great place to visit, especially a small one. The environment is usually friendly, interesting, and there are lots of kids to watch and play with (although storeowners may not like this description!).

Here's a sample dialogue: A toddler asks, "Can I go to the toy store?" or "Can I go to the park?" The parent says, "Yes, we can *visit* the toy store," or "We can *visit* the park." Just as the importance of saying your child's name every day helps to reinforce his or her identity, the word *visit* reinforces the concept that sharing, playing, and going somewhere do not necessarily mean getting something. You must also tell your child in advance that you will not be able to buy a toy this time.

If this is the first time you are reading this, you're probably thinking, "This author is incredibly naive. I'm going to walk into a toy store, tell my 2-year-old we're just visiting, and he won't throw a tantrum when he leaves empty-handed. Come on, I want my money back for this book." Well, I understand, but let's look at why it works. Assuming you've been applying these principles, the trust that has been established between you and your child is now strong enough to allow you to set limits without fear of any tantrums. Your child may complain, but that is entirely different from a tantrum. So next time say, "Yes, let's go visit a toy store" instead of "Let's go to the toy store." Gradually, you will begin to see the dramatic effect this statement will have on your son or

> Just as the importance of saying your child's name every day helps to reinforce his or her identity, the word *visit* reinforces the concept that sharing, playing, and going somewhere do not necessarily mean getting something.

daughter's *expectations*. In time, it will mean to your child he or she is "going but not getting."

The same principle of giving advance notice applies when it is time to leave. For example, just before it's time to leave, it's advisable to give your child a few minutes of *advance notice* (several times), 3 or 4 minutes apart, so he can begin to prepare himself to leave. You say, "Tommy, we have to go in 5 minutes." When 2 minutes is left you say, "2 more minutes, Tommy." When 2 minutes passes you then say, "Our visit time is up, it's time to leave. We have to go now, Tommy . . . we're just visiting. I know you understand. We will come back and visit again. Everything will be waiting for you." (Pause and wait for response.) "I know you *wish* you could take the race car with you. You wish you could take the whole store with you. Today we are visiting. Now it's time to leave."

If we examine this process, you will see we first gave an advance notice of the time. Adults as well as children do not like to be abruptly stopped in the middle of something interesting or fun. Giving advance notice about when something will happen shows your child you value time and mean what you say. Second, by repeating the theme of *visiting*, you put the emphasis on exactly that part of the experience and begin to establish future expectations. Third, by giving your child in fantasy what he can't have in reality ("I wish you could take the race car with you"), you are showing him understanding. This diminishes his anger and encourages cooperation. Children feel demeaned when adults make fun of their wishes and deny them outright.

Slow and sincere repetition is critical to the communication process and will also help your toddler to relax. In addition, you have told your child you will come back on another day—always try to keep your word. Ginott suggests that parents "never say the

word *promise,* as it encourages unrealistic expectations [and sug-
gests] the unpromised word is not trustworthy."

After about three or four months of hearing you call these
trips *visits,* your child's response will become more positive and
trusting. Although this may sound too good to be true, it will
work. However, keep in mind that no idea works in an isolated
vacuum. These principles are cumulative. They will work for you,
too! The point is this: If a toddler is taught to understand that
trips are visits, in time he won't have the expectation of "getting
something."

Talk Slowly

ALTHOUGH I am not an advocate of television as a learning tool
for toddlers and young children, there is one show that consistently demonstrates superb child communication skills. The PBS
television show *Mr. Rogers' Neighborhood* combines all the necessary elements to allow children to follow the storytelling themes.
Mr. Rogers' slow, deliberate, and single-theme ideas give children
the opportunity to fully understand what he is saying. He uses
words he knows children understand, and when he introduces a
new word he takes time to explain the meaning. He also talks
about children's feelings as they relate to the show's theme. He
talks about how friendship, school, travel, family, and the whole
world in general relate to children's lives and their world. He
rarely gets ahead of them. Although he has a television audience
of millions, he makes everyone who is watching feel as though he
is talking *only to him or her.*

Because the show is filmed with only one studio camera (no
quick cutaways), each child can follow Mr. Rogers around his

neighborhood without feeling rushed and confused. Child psychologist Dorothy Baruch's philosophy of parenting exactly mirrors the premise behind *Mr. Rogers' Neighborhood:* "Chief among the things that matter most are *not* the best toys or places, but rather the imagination of the hand, the heart, and the head. In the end, it is the adult's eagerness for becoming attuned to how a child feels that determines their connection. Here the major assets are the ear that listens, the eye that watches, the open mind, and a true, deep, and earnest wish to develop sympathy and accord."

Parents Must Remain Relaxed

CHILDREN CAN feel when you are rushing them. Here again, the right attitude will help give you the right perspective. A toddler determines his or her trust in part by your patience and consistency. Over time, as you demonstrate the right attitude, your toddler or child will see you more relaxed and confident. This will help your child manage his or her frustrations better because you are managing yours.

> *The right message promotes*
> *the right behavior.*

7

Dangerous "No's"

WHAT'S MORE NATURAL for a parent than protecting his or her child? Even before you bring your beautiful newborn home, chances are you've already thought about "baby-proofing" your house. Making your home safe is job number one. Along with that responsibility comes knowing how to react in front of your child when she is faced with real danger or with what you may perceive as danger. This chapter's focus is on how to prevent a future accident when you've got to teach your child the lessons of real danger.

It's interesting how toddlers always want the real thing rather than a toy. Boy, do they know the difference! You give them a toy phone—they prefer the real one. You give them a plastic hammer—they'll find the real one. You give them a small plastic fork—they want your big, sharp, stainless-steel one. When Dad is shaving, they want the real razor. This is no coincidence. Every day they see you using and enjoying these things.

Potential danger is all around us, but we must not overreact to it. That is why, when we have to say "no," we should try (when possible) to demonstrate the consequences. Children are more accepting of a limit when they understand and become part of the explanation. "Tommy, feel how hot the cup is." As the ancient Chinese saying goes, "When I hear, I forget; when I see, I remember; when I do, I understand.

This is a difficult subject to tackle because of the visceral feelings that surface when we talk about danger. As parents, we need to consciously decide whether we explain and demonstrate danger to our toddlers or whether we avoid the subject entirely by just pulling a child away and telling him "no." The problem with continually pulling them away is that this causes children's curiosity to build up. Many unfortunate accidents happen when a toddler somehow finds a way to get to an object that was always taken away, concealed, or never explained. When a child does not understand the consequences of certain types of danger, her curiosity can be unquenchable. If you think an explanation is unnecessary, think again.

So what is the appropriate age to talk to children about danger? If 7-month-old Artie is crawling toward an electrical outlet, his dad may shout, "No, Artie, that's dangerous." Such a command to Artie at this age has no meaning whatsoever. Nor should it. It is far healthier to quietly pick up Artie and place him somewhere safer. It's best not to make a moment an event. Of course, a parent should react differently to a 20-month-old holding a pair of sharp scissors. Here, an explanation and demonstration may very well prevent a later accident.

Teach Understanding, Not Fear

CONFRONTING DANGER, like most things in life, is not quite as simple as one might think. Although we want to avoid danger, we must not teach our toddlers and children to fear it. We must teach them to understand it. Indeed, sometimes we should let them closely examine it under our supervision. Even though these ideas and explanations are too advanced to be grasped by an infant-turned-toddler, it's not too soon for the parent to begin practicing this kind of thinking. The parent is the first and primary source for a child to learn how to manage his curiosity and his fears. The way you respond to danger with your physical and facial expressions, tone, and emotions will teach your toddler not only how to feel about it, but what to think about it. It is essential that you use a calm but very serious manner when explaining and demonstrating the potential danger of an object.

"Dana, let Mommy show you how it works."
"Paul, feel how hot the toast is."
"Tommy, feel how sharp the knife is."

Yes, there is a degree of risk here, but only in relation to the degree of danger. You may think at this point, "Hey, wait a minute, why should I take any risk with my toddler? I'll take the object away and that's the end of it." That may be the end of the object, but not of the danger. Life is full of danger and you're not always going to be there to "take it away." A better lesson to teach would be how to understand danger. A 2-year-old has an enormous capacity to intuit if you provide the right tools.

As an adult, you know that being frightened or having fears clouds one's reasoning. In short, it encourages panic. Panic can be more dangerous than the danger itself. A startled, panicked expression can scare a child. "Emily, look out! That can fall on you!" "Todd, quick, put that down!" Parents must be careful not to shout or run too fast to their

> Although we want to avoid danger, we must not teach our toddlers and children to fear it. We must teach them to understand it.

toddlers when they are in a dangerous situation. Unfortunately, many times the toddler will react to the parent's panic and do the exact opposite of the parent's shouted instructions. This often causes the accident!

Early Patterned Responses

JEROME KAGAN, an eminent developmental psychologist at Harvard University, confirms that the temperament of an infant is shaped in part by how a parent may overprotect or underprotect in an environment of stress or danger. Author and psychologist Dan Goleman elaborates on Kagan's point of view in his book *Emotional IQ*. Kagan says, "There is something learned when a baby has his steady crawl toward what seems to him an intriguing object (but to his mother a dangerous one) interrupted by her warning, 'Get away from that!' The infant is suddenly forced to deal with a mild uncertainty. The repetition of this challenge hundreds of times during the first year of life gives the infant continual rehearsals, in small doses, of meeting the unexpected in life. For fearful children that is precisely the encounter that has to be mastered, and those manageable doses are just right for learning the lesson."

Naturally, thoughtful caution is prudent, and parents must practice greater understanding in determining what is really dangerous and what is not dangerous. If we are completely honest with ourselves, we would acknowledge that we interfere too soon with our infants' and toddlers' explorations not because they are doing something dangerous, but because we lack patience and are not in the mood to remain alert while we watch them. At first glance, being patient appears to be a passive and easy activity, more of a waiting game. However, on closer examination we discover that patience really requires work. If you are patient, the toddler will probably explore more, which makes for more cleanup. Just watching a toddler is work because you have to remain so alert. Making the conscious effort to think before interfering too soon is what each parent must do each day to encourage his or her toddler's spirit.

Real Danger Versus Perceived Danger

TWENTY MONTHS is a good age to begin teaching your child the process of recognizing and demonstrating the consequences of dangerous situations or actions. When you take your time and avoid overreacting, your child will learn how to understand the danger and the consequences. This early foundation in thinking and practice will result in visible benefits after about six months.

As we examine the real danger of everyday objects, such as scissors, knives, electrical outlets, fireplaces, matches, and more, you will soon see that danger can be minimized but not eliminated from daily life. A child holding a closed box of matches should elicit an entirely different reaction from you than a child examining a single match. For one thing, a single match can't be easily lit, but it can be easily swallowed. A 22-month-old toddler sitting and holding a pair of scissors with a parent in front of him is entirely different from a toddler running with a pair of scissors in her hand. I am not suggesting that a toddler should ever have such an object in his hand. However, if by accident a child manages to get hold of one, the parent has the perfect opportunity to teach about possible dangers before putting the object away in the drawer.

Eleven-month-old Emily was just beginning to walk when her father saw her in the living room, pressed cheek-to-cheek with the big TV screen. Immediately her father said, "No, Emily, you're too close," and within seconds Emily was whisked away. What can we learn from this story? Where was the danger? Was she watching TV for hours like this? No. Could the sound of the TV damage her ears? Not for 3 seconds. Was she damaging her eyes? Unlikely. Here, the real danger was based not on a real fear such as radiation exposure but rather on an overreaction to a few seconds too close to a television. Her parent's watchful eye was all that was necessary for this toddler for those few seconds. Most likely, the large pictures and booming sound would have startled her and caused her to back up. If that didn't happen, then the parent should have intervened.

> As parents make daily judgments as to what is real danger and what is perceived danger, their need to protect should be balanced with their infant's or toddler's need to explore.

However, hot stoves, open knife drawers, street traffic, open railings, chemical products, and much more represent real dangers that should always remain inaccessible to the child and remembered by the parent. As parents make daily judgments as to what is real danger and what is perceived danger, their need to protect should be balanced with their infant's or toddler's need to explore.

Three Common Situations

BE SURE that your toddler is ready to listen and focus on the potential danger you are about to explain; otherwise, postpone the demonstration until a later time. If you have never previously demonstrated or talked specifically about why something can be dangerous, begin a trust-building exercise by taking out a relatively innocuous object, such as a pencil with a point. Show your child how sharp it is and how can pierce a piece of paper. Touch it to your finger first, then to you child's. Children can sense when you include them in a serious discussion and will pay more attention in a different kind of way. Your slow, deliberate, and calm manner will convey the importance of your words and help your child to focus on what you are saying and showing. Keep your explanation and/or demonstration simple at all times.

The Table Story

Doug, a 2-year-old, has managed to climb on top of the kitchen table, 3 feet above the slate floor.

DOUG: "Mommy, look at me!"

MOTHER: "Yes, I see you, Doug. I see you. The table is not for climbing. Doug, look down, see how far the floor is? Now look up, see how high up you are?"

DOUG: "Yeah." (He immediately grasps the drama of how high up he is because his mother got him to look both ways.)

MOTHER: (Holding an apple) "Look at the apple when I drop it on the floor."

DOUG: (Focuses on the lesson at hand and sees his mother's expression: This is very serious.)

MOTHER: (Picks up the apple slowly from the floor) "Look, Doug, the apple is bruised from the fall. This could happen to you if you were to fall. That would hurt. It's very, very dangerous. Doug, I know you understand. I know you understand."

DOUG: "Down, Mommy."

MOTHER: "Yes, Doug. Mommy will help you down. It's a good idea to come down."

Lesson: Climbing high is dangerous.
Message: Doug is smart. Doug knows when to ask for help. Doug can reason.

The Lamp Story

Brian, 26 months old, was pulling the cord of the floor lamp. He did not understand that if he pulled with all his weight the lamp would fall.

FATHER: (Quickly moving next to him, also holding the cord so there could be no danger of the lamp falling.) "Brian, do you see what the cord is attached to? Look, Brian, look at the cord. Look at what it's attached to." (Dad points to the base of the lamp.) "Brian, do you see it? It is attached to the lamp."

BRIAN: "Yeah."

FATHER: "Look, it's attached to the lamp. You see the cord attached to the lamp, don't you? Brian, look what happens if you pull on the cord." (Dad is now pulling the lamp down to the floor in slow motion to demonstrate the consequences.) "Whoa!" (Doug's father struggles to keep the lamp from hitting the floor—a little acting helps.) "Brian, this is danger-ous—very dangerous."

BRIAN: "Yeah, dangerous." (The expression on his face re-mains serious and alert. Brian now knows this is not a game and appreciates the information.)

Lesson: You need to look at what you're playing with.

Message: I respect Brian. Brian is intelligent. I trust Brian.

The Scissors Story

When Alexis, a 20-month-old toddler, points to a pair of scissors on top of the table and says, "I want this," she is ready for you to help her understand what scissors are and why they can be dan-gerous. Remember, whether your toddler has an extensive vocab-ulary or a more limited one, her comprehension level will be greater than her words.

> Remember, whether your toddler has an exten-sive vocabulary or a more limited one, her comprehension level will be greater than her words.

FATHER: "Alexis, do you want to see it?"

ALEXIS: "Yes, Daddy." (Father squats down slowly to show Alexis the tip of the scissors.)

FATHER: "Alexis, look at the tip of the scissors, see the point? Watch me touch the point." (Uses palm of hand) "Wow, that's sharp!" (A little acting helps here.) "Alexis, would you like to feel the point?"

ALEXIS: "Yes." (Father slowly puts the point in Alexis's palm.)

FATHER: "Feel how sharp the point is?"

ALEXIS: "Yes, sharp."

FATHER: "Alexis, this is not a toy. It is for cutting things like rope or paper. It is not a toy. You understand that, don't you Alexis? It's very sharp!"

ALEXIS: "Yes, sharp."

FATHER: "The scissors belong in the drawer. Let's put them in the drawer together."

Lesson: A pair of scissors is not a toy. Scissors can be dangerous.

Message: I trust Alexis. I respect Alexis. Alexis is responsible.

You can be sure Alexis now knows the seriousness of the situation and feels the respect you are showing her. This is a giant step forward in building mutual trust between the parent and child. With less dangerous objects (cameras, Mom's makeup, etc.), try to allow your toddler the experience of getting the object back after you've explained how to use it (or how *not* to use it!). "Bonnie, you can hold it but not play with it." For an adult this small act may seem to hold no value, but for a child it will have value. Although her impulse may be to play with it, watch how she tries to regulate herself and learn self-control. This subtle but critical gesture is what reinforces the trust and confidence you are building. When she does transgress, apply the same principles we have talked about throughout this book. If she asks to repeat this exercise again on another day or even hours later, it is advisable to do so, as long as she holds the object and does not play with it.

Learning about danger offers the opportunity to replace fear with understanding. When I hear, I forget; when I see, I remember; when I do, I understand.

8

7 Steps to Saying "No"

MANY PARENTS TURN down a request from their child by saying the word "no" with such fervor that they impart the feeling that they never really even considered it. "No, Tommy, I can't play with you!" or "Samantha, no ice cream!" That tense response pushes the child further away from compliance. Saying "no" in one step completely discounts the process of mutual respect. The message to your child is, "I don't have to listen to you, you have to listen to me." From a practical point of view that may be true. From a motivational and developmental point of view, it precludes your child wanting to abide you. This approach doesn't mean you enter a debate each time you can't do what they ask. It does mean it should feel as though a dialogue took place, even if it only lasts 20 seconds. The key is to keep your message simple and not waiver on the limit you set.

Saying "no" properly is not hard to do. The hard part is the repetition required. The parent must stay focused on the seven following steps. It's a learning process that will span about 3 months before the communication between the parent and child is comfortable and somewhat predictable.

Still, these seven steps should not be viewed as a fairy-tale method that will instantly stop all misbehaviors. They will, however, give every child a solid head start for learning better how to self-regulate. Do not worry if you forget or apply them out of sequence. What is important are the principles.

Depending on the relationship between the parent and child, each child will respond uniquely. Some will respond faster, others slower, but in the end this method will minimize conflict and resentment.

Many books and professional commentaries on the subject of child discipline allow for such a wide range of differing opinions that experts in the field wind up crossing their fingers and hoping for the best. Then, regardless of what behavior is demonstrated, they label it "normal" or "a stage." This doesn't have to be. The goal is to socialize your child through a communication process without hurting his emotional well-being. The principles in this book for teaching self-control and enforcing limits are proven and time-tested. Let them work for you!

Before you begin applying the 7-Step Method, let me stress the importance of not succumbing to any family or outside pressure. You must not focus on how it might look or sound to other people when you are saying these expressions to your toddler or child. Read this entire chapter before you start using the 7-Step Method. The greater your understanding and context of it, the greater your success will be.

The 7-Step Method for Saying "No"

THESE PRINCIPLES minimize conflict and allow a child to more easily choose a different outcome*:

1. Confirm the request.
2. Provide facts.

*Don't be concerned if you sometimes mix up the order.

3. Affirm feelings.

4. Allow in fantasy what you can't in reality.

5. Demonstrate what you mean (when possible).

6. Instill confidence.

7. Offer choices.

Step 1: Confirm the Request

This display of active listening confirms to your toddler that you understand and you respect what he is saying. No one wants to be ignored. This is particularly important because his vocabulary may be limited and his words may be garbled. By repeating his request, you are also showing confidence in his ability to communicate clearly by translating what you know he is trying to say. Repeat his request at least twice. It will also help him remain open to hearing the rest of your answer, rather than just closing down.

> Active listening confirms to your toddler that you understand and you respect what he is saying. This is particularly important because his vocabulary may be limited and his words may be garbled.

Examples:

"Yes, Bobby, you want an ice cream."

"Yes, Lilly, you want to go outside."

"Yes, Todd, you want to go to the park."

Step 2: Provide Facts

Resist the temptation of saying the word *no*. It's more effective to express disapproval with strong and intense feelings: "Alex, I won't allow you to hit Robert. Robert is not for hitting. Use your words if you want to tell him you're angry; tell him you're angry! But Robert is not for hitting and Alex, you're not for hitting, either." For more common acts of misbehavior, just provide information about why something can't be done: "The repairman will be here in 5 minutes. Mommy needs to be in the house when the man comes." "Lilly, the rain will make your clothes all wet. The wetness will make you cold." "Yes, Todd, you want to go to the park at night. But nighttime is for sleeping." Keep your explanation simple and to the point. This discussion will make your child feel like he is a part of the process, instead of feeling invisible and powerless. However, never debate. You will most likely need to repeat your explanation many times. During this time, try to remain consistent in maintaining the key points in order to give your toddler or child a chance to focus on these details. If your child asks why or responds with other questions, do not take this as a sign of stubbornness or stalling. The more questions children ask, the more they are learning how to gather information and arrive at their own answers and conclusions. This is very self-satisfying and teaches the process of reasoning and self-control.

Examples:

"Alex, I won't allow you to hit Robert. Robert is not for hitting."

"Lilly, the rain will make your clothes all wet. The wetness will make you cold."

"Yes, Todd, you want to go to the park at night. But nighttime is for sleeping."

Step 3: Affirm Their Feelings

Toddlers and children must have the freedom to express their feelings without being judged. When you allow them that freedom, they are more open to hearing why you are saying "no." Although they will still resist and push limits, they will also learn to trust you with their real feelings. Over time they will push less and please more. Repeat your affirmation more than once.

Examples:

"Yes, Bobby, I know you're angry that there's no ice cream. I see you're really, really angry!"

"You're sad that we are not going outside. It's disappointing. You really wanted to go."

"Todd, I see you're angry at Mommy for not taking you to the park. You don't like staying home."

Step 4: Allow in Fantasy What You Can't Give in Reality

Even as adults we sometimes wish for better circumstances when we are faced with rejection or problems. It's part of life, and children are no different than us in that respect. Granting them their wishes (if only in fantasy) shows empathy and respect. Such expressions of empathy must be said with genuine sensitivity and sincerity.

Examples:

"Bobby, I wish the entire freezer were filled with ice cream."

"Lilly, you wish all your friends could play with you now."

"Todd, I wish it was light out so you could play basketball all day."

Step 5: Demonstrate What You Mean (When Possible)

Demonstrating the consequences is an important key to your child's understanding and acceptance of why you have to say "no." (Some drama also helps!) By showing how something works or what happens if something drops, you are teaching understanding without fear. It's worth yet again repeating the ancient saying, "When I hear, I forget; when I see, I remember; when I do, I understand." Take your time and demonstrate the possible consequences to your child at least twice. This imparts the message "You are intelligent and I trust you."

> Demonstrating the consequences is an important key to your child's understanding and acceptance of why you have to say "no." Take your time and demonstrate the possible consequences to your child at least twice. This imparts the message "You are intelligent and I trust you."

In situations where you had to take an object away (Mom's makeup bag, a camera, etc.), let your child now hold it again with new clear limits and information. "Carol, you can hold it in your hands and look at it, but you may not push the buttons." This helps build trust and self-confidence and provides children the chance to act on what they have just heard and learned. The message is, "I know you understand. You will do the right thing." Of course if she persists and violates that trust, you must take the object back. However, your tone should never be punishing. You say, "You made the choice, now I must take it back."

Examples:

"Bobby, let's look in the freezer together. There is no more ice cream. We ate it all."

"Lilly, look what happens to our hair and feet in the rain." (It only takes a few seconds.)

"Todd, look what happens when I throw you the ball in the dark. Look how hard it is to see. "

Step 6: Instill Confidence

This is the part of the conversation where you build confidence. By telling your child you have confidence in him to do the right thing, you are showing him respect and promoting good behavior. These expressions should be said sincerely and with a very positive attitude. Repeat your confidence in him more than once, perhaps in a different way.

Examples:

"Bobby, I know you understand now."

"Lilly, I see you understand now how rain can make you wet."

"Todd, it's hard to play in the dark. You understand that now."

Step 7: Offer Choices

Nobody likes to be forced into only one action. Your toddler or child is no different. Being provided a choice makes a child feel as though he has control over himself and his world. It empowers him and helps develop his powers of reasoning. In addition, your child is learning responsibility through the decision-making process. During these early years, only two choices should be available when the parent is presenting options. More than two choices will confuse and encourage debate. It's okay to repeat the choices more than once. For older children, multiple choices work best.

Examples:

"Bobby, you can have a lollipop or a juice bar. The choice is yours. You make the choice."

"Lilly, you can play in the playroom or the kitchen. The choice is yours."

"Todd, you can read your books or paint. It's your choice."

Be Realistic

OF COURSE, in the beginning a 20-month-old toddler is not going to say, "Okay, Mom, I made my choice, I'll read a book." However, toddlers process significantly more vocabulary than they are able to verbalize. Over time, their comprehension will allow them to understand what you are telling them, so that if you do have to take an object away, they will feel as though they were first given the opportunity to abide. This process helps the toddler to reason and self-regulate. In about 3 months, he will feel more respected and will know you mean it when you say, "You have a choice." This will cause him either to make less of a fuss or abide by your request. These simple choices should be given each and every time you must take an object away.

When providing a choice, it is important that you recognize the value of crying or whining as a reaction. In the long run, this emphasizes the child's control over her own behavior. The parent —if she has the time—should wait out the episode. While the child is crying, the parent must remain respectful. Try not to demean or attack the child's character or personality. Don't use such phrases as, "Carol, grow up. You sound like a baby," or "Carl, I'm not going to listen to you if you keep crying." Instead, acknowledge and reflect their feelings.

Don't Give Up!

YOU MAY have to follow the 7-Step Method for about 90 days before you see results. In the beginning, it may feel awkward to keep repeating each step. You might have to keep repeating for up to 10 minutes or longer when you start. Stay with it. Allow your

> Allow your toddler or child to complain about what you're saying "no" to for as long as she wishes. Show her how you can journey through her disappointment.

toddler or child to complain about what you're saying "no" to for as long as she wishes. Show her how you can journey through her disappointment. Be comfortable with your choice of words, tailoring them to your style. Be yourself. After a few months, she will begin to understand and govern her disappointment. Your toddler or child is learning the powers of reasoning and self-control.

Using the Seven Steps

WITH A little practice, you will be able to apply the 7-Step Method automatically to any situation. The following scenarios demonstrate how natural an interchange between you and your child can sound. Speak slowly and sincerely.

Conversation #1

Eric, a 2-year-old, is crying and pointing to go outside.

MOTHER: "Eric, I see you want to play outside. Yes, Eric, we will go outside.

   Mommy is talking on the telephone and needs to finish her conversation. Mommy likes to finish what she starts. You're waiting good."

ERIC: "No! Outside."

MOTHER: "Eric, I know you wish I would stop my telephone call right now and go outside with you. I know you understand. Sometimes it's hard to wait. When I am finished we will go outside."

ERIC: (Crying)

MOTHER: "I know you wish I would stop talking. But Mommy is going to finish talking on the phone. Eric, look at the telephone. Mommy is talking on the phone. I know you understand that. I know it can be hard to wait."

ERIC: "Mommy—outside!"

MOTHER: "Eric, you can play with your toys or you can watch television. The choice is yours. You make the choice."

ERIC: (Still crying)

MOTHER: "That's okay, you want to cry. That's your choice. Sometimes it's hard to wait."

Lesson: Sometimes you have to wait for things.

Message: Mommy listens to Eric. Mommy understands Eric. Eric can make his own choices.

This example is both repetitive and realistic. It demonstrates the process rather than a happy result. Naturally, a toddler is not going to learn self-control from hearing this two or three times from a parent. However, over the next three months or so the results will be significantly more positive.

Conversation #2

Carol, a 3 1/2-year-old child, is screaming, "Ice cream, ice cream!"

MOTHER: "Carol, I see you want ice cream. Yes, you want ice cream."

CAROL: "Ice cream, Mommy."

MOTHER: "Yes, Carol, we will have ice cream after dinner. Yes, Carol, we will have ice cream after dinner."

CAROL: "Ice cream. Ice cream!"

MOTHER: "You wish you could have strawberry ice cream right now. You wish you could have ice cream all day long. Carol, you can have a rice cake or you can have some apple juice. The choice is yours. You can have a rice cake or apple juice. You make the choice."

CAROL: "No, ice cream, ice cream."

MOTHER: "Yes, I know you want ice cream. I also know you understand. I wish you could have 10 big ice creams. You have a choice, a rice cake or apple juice. You make the choice. Carol, I know you understand."

Lesson: You can't always get what you want.

Message: I understand what Carol wants. There's nothing wrong with what Carol wants. Carol has choices.

This example is also intended to be realistic. Each parent must be prepared to hear and say the same words over and over again. In time this will work.

Stay calm. Stay respectful.
Keep repeating.

9

Don't Talk Down—
Talk Up!

T HE LENGTH OF time it takes for your child to accept your "no's" is largely dependent on your style of communicating. "Talking up" to a child really means talking to him with respect. It means not talking down, not talking at, not ignoring, and certainly not talking above his or her level. As Dr. Ginott used to say, "Treat a child as though he is already the person he is capable of becoming." "Talking up" to a child will feel more relaxed and natural for you, as well as less taxing. It takes more energy to talk down to your child than it does to talk with him or her. So, at what age should parents begin this kind of dialogue with their child? You should start on day one! Of course, I'm not suggesting that an infant understands the meaning behind this manner of talking with him; rather, I am suggesting that doing so gives the parent an early start in practicing this kind of thinking and talking.

Don't Worry About Intelligence

RESPECT SHOULD be the cornerstone of how you talk with your child. Speaking to your child with respect develops the emotional and intellectual foundation for trust between the parent and child. Although many parents focus on their child's intellect during this period (perhaps because of the unnatural competitiveness that society has reinforced), the real focus should be on behavior. It's worth repeating what Dr. Arnold Gesell said: "The mind manifests itself." What this means is that the individual intelligence for each child cannot be accelerated faster than its inherent rate. Author and psychologist David Elkind writes in his book *The Hurried Child* that pushing a child too early to read regardless of his development can result in the child's diminished enjoyment in reading later on.

Renowned Swiss developmental psychologist Jean Piaget goes as far as suggesting that children should not be taught abstract symbol systems (such as those found in mathematics and reading) until about age 5. Despite the fact that strong research supports and demonstrates that children achieve developmental readiness well before this age, a parent should not ignore a child's emotional readiness. At this point, parents may want to rethink their emphasis and expectations regarding their child's intellectual development. So take the pressure off yourself and your toddler, put the flash cards away, and concentrate on behavior, not intelligence. As in all human communication, overlapping characteristics are found in all developmental stages. Within these stages are four important characteristics of communication: speed, content, repetition, and attitude.

The Infant (Up to 12 Months)

During the first 12 months of your infant's life, the speed of your conversations should be natural—the way you talk with your family and friends. There is no need to slow down your speech. That will come at the next stage of your baby's development (about 15 months). Your infant is now processing the rhythm of your natural speech in addition to continuing to develop her own muscular and neurological systems. She's listening to the gentle sound of your voice and associating those sounds as her primary source of physical and emotional comfort.

Next, the content of what you should be saying to your infant may surprise you. Because sounds have more of an effect than words, this is a good point in our discussion to distinguish between baby sounds and baby talk. Baby sounds are the repetitive vowels and consonants that we coo to our infants to make them smile and laugh—"Da da-gaga-babeeda"—and are always playful. Your infant is learning how and when to respond to both your voice and face. Parents prefer to make these baby sounds as they are easy to say and fun to do. In addition to making those fun baby sounds, be sure to talk to your infant as you normally do. Emphasize content, vocabulary, and tone. "Mommy is going in the car." "Timmy, look at the dog." "Bobby, say good-bye to my friend Sandy."

Unfortunately, some parents and adults feel foolish having a natural conversation with a 9-month-old infant. Part of what makes adults sometimes feel foolish is the lack of reaction or the blank-stare response they can get from an infant. Parents can help minimize their discomfort and self-consciousness by reminding themselves that they are teaching the process of language and conversation.

Parents should also try not to describe an infant's negative behavior in front of the child when carrying on a conversation with a third person. Try not to say things such as, "Allison is a cranky baby," or "Jill is a shy baby" within earshot of the child. These negative expressions, over time, are processed by the infant. Moreover, a parent's pattern of communicating become more serious when they carry over into toddlerhood.

When parents are embarrassed by their toddler's lack of a proper response to another person, they often respond with an immediate apology for their toddler's behavior. "I don' t know why Teddy is so shy." "Katie, you're being rude when you don't say hello." "Tommy, are you going to continue acting like a monster today?" At this point, the toddler will become embarrassed and will likely continue to act out on what he hears. This is the meaning behind the expression "You are what you hear."

> Parents may want to rethink their emphasis and expectations regarding their child's intellectual development. So take the pressure off yourself and your toddler, put the flash cards away, and concentrate on behavior, not intelligence.

Alternative positive expressions in such situations may be, "I see you don't want to talk now. Maybe later." "You're having difficulty controlling your anger. I know you can stop." If, however, parents are aware enough early on of their tendency to unwittingly embarrass their child, these patterns can be prevented. Being aware early is the key. The right attitude supports your infant's feeling of well-being. It reflects how you feel about the giving of yourself each day.

The Toddler (18 Months to 3 Years)

The speed, content, repetition, and attitude of your dialogue with your toddler should change dramatically once she reaches 15 to 18 months. First, stop all the baby talk! "Does Lilly want a ba-ba?" "Does Booby boo see doggie?" Some parents add the suffix *y* to

their child's first name: "Good boy, Mikey," "Put it here, Greggy."
Although this may sound cute and loving to the parent, the toddler hears his or her name differently. For a toddler, baby talk reinforces the feelings that she is still a baby. The toddler will mimic
baby names and baby talk instead of learning real words. More importantly, when you use baby talk, you are talking down to a toddler, not up! In addition, it encourages toddlers to use other
abbreviated words, which results in parents having to correct them
later. Although many toddlers may say an abbreviated version of a
word ("ruff-ruff" or "ba-ba"), they should still hear it pronounced
correctly: "Look, Timmy a big dog," or "Do you want a bottle
now?" Baby talk directly conflicts with a child's own natural development and need for autonomy. This is a time for rapid vocabulary expansion. When baby talk continues into the toddler years,
behavioral maturity will almost always be delayed. Every parent
should look for ways to expand a toddler's vocabulary.

During these early years, parents must be careful not to imi-
tate the mispronunciations of their toddler's words, believing that
this somehow shows understanding. You should not repeat, "Yes,
Billy, it's a bawoon." In fact, this will confuse him more, because
in his mind he will think he is saying the word correctly. Some
parents unwittingly continue to correct their toddler: "No, Billy,
you mean balloon, not bawoon." This unnecessary correction de-
means your toddler and encourages him to begin to mumble his
words for fear of correction, and he may even begin to retreat
from daily conversations. In addition, it penalizes a child for
something he has no control over: his vocal sound and tongue
placements. Rather than drawing attention to his mispronuncia-
tion, repeat it correctly: "Yes, Billy, it is a balloon."

It also helps to slow down your tempo to less than half the
speed that you normally talk. In the beginning this may seem

awkward or silly, but you must remember the goal here is not to see how many new words you can pack into a sentence, but rather to connect with your toddler on her level—both intellectually and emotionally. At the toddler stage, slow down your tempo to less than half the speed that you normally talk. Just because your toddler may have an advanced vocabulary and can follow your directions does not always mean she feels good about how you rush your instructions or conversations. Talk slowly and try to pay attention and respond to each of her vocalizations. This way, your child will feel not that you are ahead of her but rather that you are in step with her. This is critical to building trust. As a parent, you may find the pace too slow, but just look at your toddler's face and you will find her focused and relaxed as you talk with her.

> In the beginning this may seem awkward or silly, but you must remember the goal here is not to see how many new words you can pack into a sentence, but rather to connect with your toddler on her level—both intellectually and emotionally.

Remember when you took your first foreign-language class? After about a year you were just getting comfortable with the sound and the rhythm. Didn't you feel more relaxed and trusting with a teacher who spoke slowly and allowed you the time to understand? Well, it's the same thing for your 2-year old, only more so!

In addition, consider offering your toddler feedback on the emotions she shows you. You may say, "Annie, are you angry at Daddy?" or when your toddler is smiling happily, you can say, "I see you're feeling happy." When you label emotions for a child you help her begin to identify and classify her own moods and feelings. In his book *First Feelings*, psychiatrist and author Stanley Greenspan supports this premise by saying, "It's not unusual for a 2-year old to giggle over a sad event or look at you with a mean face and then smile." Toddlers are just learning how to categorize and internalize their emotions. As parents you can help them navigate, label, and understand their feelings.

Tell Me Again!

YOU KNOW from reading books to your child how much he enjoys hearing the same story, in exactly the same way, a thousand times. That's how he likes to learn—it provides a part of his daily routine and security. He knows he's learning by remembering the answers he has heard before. This helps his memory and mastery. That's why it is quite common for a toddler to repeat the same question or request 20 times. "Daddy, what's this?" "Mommy, why is the tree here?" Parents should not get frustrated with a child's incessant repetition of questions. They should correctly answer him every time. "Darren, this is a scooter." "Annie, the tree was planted here." By staying with your toddler step for step, question for question, you are establishing the trust and respect he is seeking.

Most toddlers already know the answers to many of their questions, but they are repeating the answers to themselves to flex their memories. They are also testing your level of interest. This is a critical parent test to pass. Most parents begin to ignore their child or act annoyed after the third or fourth question. Somehow they think their toddler is being willfully obnoxious. "Tyler, how many times are you going to ask the same question?" "I already told you what that is!" This kind of response inhibits a child's motivation to inquire and acquire. The "question-asking stage" is an important stage and should be regarded as a child's serious effort to extend his vocabulary and gain information. One psychologist and researcher tracked his own 3-year-old in terms of how many questions a day he asked. He counted 176 questions. I tried it with my 2^1/2-year-old and counted 127 questions that day. Try to stay even-tempered when you respond and respectful with your answers. Repetition is essential in building a trusting relationship as well as helping a child's development and motivation for learning and practice.

> The "question-asking stage" is an important stage and should be regarded as a child's serious effort to extend his vocabulary and gain information.

When you explain your reason for saying "no," it is best to keep your reason simple. Try to fight the impulse to make explanations longer or more interesting. Toddlers take delight in their ability to focus on the simplicity of what you are saying. At the conclusion of this exchange, a parent may tell his or her toddler, "Thank you, Todd, for understanding," or "Thank you, Anne, for waiting." This gives what you are saying a mature overtone and promotes more "big boy/big girl" behavior. Parents sometimes tend to reserve the words *thank you* for teaching manners only.

In addition, when you want to set a limit or tell your child to abide, do not use the word *please*. Do not say, "Please, Carol, it's time for bed now. Your five minutes are up," or "Please, Bobby, the scissors belong in the drawer. Please, put them back now." Toddlers (as well as young children) respond to the word *please* as an invitation not to listen. It carries with it an undertone of begging. Children will then tend to believe you're not that serious and will purposefully drag out their misbehavior.

Unfortunately, some parents who believe they are modeling good manners are confusing politeness with firmness. A parent who says, "Carol, please pass the rolls" is demonstrating good manners and politeness. For times when firmness is required, it is more effective to say, "Carol, I expect you to put that back," or "Carol, I won't let you push your sister Madeline, and I won' t let Madeline push you, either."

The "Hello, I'm Here" Syndrome

BRIAN, $2^{1}/2$ years old, was sitting in a circle along with other toddlers and mothers at a "Mommy and Me" class. As part of the program, at the end of every class the leader tells each mother what she has observed about some of the toddlers during the past 90 minutes. "Bobby didn't want to play today, right, Bobby?" "Tammy had all this extra energy, so she was climbing a lot today." "Kevin wasn't hungry at snack time." "Brian was quiet and wanted to be read to." Unfortunately, the teacher took very little notice of the toddlers' expressions and embarrassment as she went around the room. Not all toddlers like their behavior to be on display.

Many educators would argue that this process teaches socialization. I would argue that this approach encourages polarization. It places a judgment on children's activity and encourages them to compare themselves with others. A comparison is far more powerful if it comes from the child's observation of others and not from the pronouncements of the adult in charge. That's why many children will learn toilet training from their friends and peers at preschool. Here they can talk about it and watch each other. They do not have to endure daily adult announcements in front of others such as, "Bobby didn't want to go to the bathroom today," or "He went to the bathroom only once." If the teacher wanted to encourage Bobby to feel better about himself in terms of potty training (or any other kind of behavior), the teacher should have first quietly asked Bobby if she could tell his Mom about his bathroom habits today. That small question builds big trust!

Larry and Dori (both 4 years old) were greeted early in the morning by their preschool teacher, who said, "Hi, Larry. I like your sneakers today. Hi, Dori. I like your shirt." Larry responded with a big smile. Dori withdrew. These are almost standard greetings from counselors and teachers who feel this flattery is a nice icebreaker when greeting a youngster. Don't be surprised if more often than not children put their heads down or entirely ignore the compliment. One reason may be that physical compliments can often embarrass young children as they search for a response. Another reason, and perhaps not as obvious, is that the child may not have picked out the article of clothing. Sometimes a parent or caregiver will insist the child wear something that matches or looks cute when the child did not want to wear it. Then comes the unwelcome greeting, "Wow, Dori, I like your shirt." A safer acknowledgment would be, "Hi, Dori. I'm happy to see you today." Toddlers and children don't require compliments as warm-ups to conversation. They prefer to be talked to in a more honest way or, better yet, be given the time to first get comfortable.

Still, there are some parents who unwittingly degrade their toddlers right in front of them. They will say, "Oh, ignore Tommy, he's just cranky," or "Darren is shy." Demeaning, embarrassing, and rejecting expressions are understood by the toddler. Over time, humiliating expressions will play a role in shaping his or her personality. Such expressions make children feel invisible and start the pattern of self-fulfilling prophecies.

Four-year-old Eric was with his parents in a restaurant when his parents' friends came over to the table. When his mother's friend asked how Eric was doing, the mother said, "Oh, he's doing fine. Eric likes his new piano lessons but he is still not ready for those swimming lessons yet. You should see him play, he's so cute." This made Eric feel both invisible and embarrassed. He had never thought of himself as cute when he played the piano. He worked hard at it. As for the swimming lessons, he remembered his older brother making fun of him when he first tried. It would have been

> Demeaning, embarrassing, and rejecting expressions are understood by the toddler. Over time, humiliating expressions will play a role in shaping his or her personality. Such expressions make children feel invisible and start the pattern of self-fulfilling prophecies.

better if Eric's mom asked permission to speak about his activities or, at the very least, said, "Eric, I was just about to tell Mrs. Johnson how hard you have been practicing piano."

Too Close Too Soon

INVASION OF privacy is usually a topic discussed and reserved for teenagers and adults. Actually, it begins in early infancy. It's not uncommon to watch an infant being turned over, without warning or any advance cue, to someone else: a caregiver, friend, or another family member. Without a proper warning, most infants will react uneasily. Even an infant can gently and properly be alerted to this change before it happens. "Alan, Aunt Marla wants to hold you now." At this point the child will look to Aunt Marla's face and her words for reassurance. If he doesn't find it, he won't want to go. Another example of this can be seen when a parent is in the supermarket and friends or strangers extend their hands to a child's face, bottom, hair, hands, and so on, all while saying "hello." This often occurs without any advance cue or permission. Early educator Jeanette Galambos Stone points out how some adults who talk with young children adopt an extra sweet voice. It is high-pitched and sticky and sounds phony to everybody, especially to the children. It invites false answers and tuning out. Some adults take on a let's-be-pals voice. However, it is too superficial and intimate. Children cannot trust such adults to mean what they say.

Michael, just 2 years old, hadn't seen his grandma in four months. When he appeared at the front door with his mom, the grandmother didn't waste a second when she lovingly whisked him in the air, held him close, and said, "How about a kiss for Grandma?" He had no time for adjustment, reflection, or reaction. Children need time to warm up and get comfortable. When Lilly, a 3-year-old, is asked by her mother's friend if she can hold her, she turns away. The mother says, "Oh, she's being shy." Whether she really is or she's just playing, it is her way of exercising her power of whom she wants to let get that close. It's a good sign for a young child to feel that sense of autonomy as she expresses her freedom regarding who touches her and who doesn't. A parent may want to narrate the child's feelings and say, "Samantha doesn't feel like being held now. Maybe later."

Every Wednesday morning David's preschool teacher blasted out a big "good morning" as David entered the room. The teacher did this with all the children as they came in the play-room. Some children feel anxious when they anticipate this type of greeting because it can place pressure on the child to respond in like manner. Just as temperaments vary, so should the style of "hello's." Even if toddlers are familiar with the people they will en-counter, each day brings a different mood and feeling. Good teachers recognize this and try to respond individually to each child. Big, loud, or even too-close-to-the-face "hello's" given by well-meaning adults, teachers, friends, or day-care workers can seem intrusive to a toddler or young child. This behavior on their part is easy to understand, as many adults want to establish a quick rapport with the child. Adults also want to satisfy their own need to have the child like them. However, sometimes a quieter "hello" or a silent little wave sends a quicker signal that you are friendly, patient, and trusting. As a rule, toddlers and children prefer to observe before they warm up and commit to anyone or anything.

The Child (3 to 5+ Years)

BETWEEN THE ages of 3 and 5 years old, your toddler starts de-veloping into a child. Talking with him now takes on a whole new meaning—for you and for him. Greater mutual understanding, fuller conversations, and a deeper exchange of ideas mark this early stage of childhood development. Now you can increase the speed of your speech quite a bit, but not to the same pace you use to talk with your friends. Even if your child is able to follow you, *don't talk that fast.* Your child will enjoy listening more when your tempo is easier to follow. By slowing down and making more eye contact, you're showing him more respect. You're telling him, "You are important." If you're not sure about this, try it and watch your child's face. Seeing is believing.

> **B**etween the ages of 3 and 5 years old, your toddler starts developing into a child. Talking with him now takes on a whole new meaning—for you and for him. Greater mutual understanding, fuller conversations, and a deeper exchange of ideas mark this early stage of childhood development.

Between Parent and Child

Now comes a long-awaited dividend: the opportunity to share with your child more advanced concepts, both intellectually and emotionally. Unlike earlier toddler stages when a trip to the supermarket can feel like a trip to a theme park, a child 4 to 6 years old can be bored with just the thought. An extensive vocabulary study by Medora Smith at the University of Iowa revealed that a 3-year-old child's vocabulary of about 900 words increases to over 2,000 words by age 5 and to about 2,500 words by age 6.

Children look for more challenging activities to which they can apply their new psychological and physical skills. Longer walks and hikes and small-scale art and science projects are good ways to deepen your emotional and intellectual relationship. Ask them to join you: "Sally, would you like to go outside and take a walk with Daddy? We can talk about what we each did today." "Todd, would you like to see how to make ice?" Listen to and hear what your child is trying to say to you and learn what he is really interested in. "Todd, I liked making those ice cubes with you. You had a good idea to use juice instead of water. I liked making ice juice with you." Todd: "Yes, Dad, it was fun and tasted good." Later, repeating what you have just talked about shows real interest and respect for what has been said and done.

At this age your child will have a thousand questions. He or she will more than likely start many of the conversations. This is proof that you have built trust with your child. Conversely, a child who usually feels challenged or ridiculed will not want to start a dialogue with the parent and will more likely wait for the parent to initiate a conversation. This is also a stage marked by a new confidence in a child's ability to express his or her intellect and logic. In the book *Playground Politics,* Stanley Greenspan provides insights into the importance of allowing a child to argue a point of view (regarding limits) that may be different from the parent's ideas. This privilege in turn will have an effect on other peer relationships. Greenspan says, "It develops capacity for logical thinking and helps make the child more determined and a more intelligent person later on in life." He stresses, "A mixture of satisfaction and necessary frustration helps a child to understand what relationships involve and teaches them to operate less in absolutes. When children have a basic sense of security in relationships, they can more easily negotiate the often boisterous interactions with their peers." So it's okay if they try to negotiate extending their limits. Parents should allow this freedom for their child's feelings and opinions while still maintaining parental limits on behavior.

By this point in time, you should be very comfortable with showing and maintaining a natural enthusiasm and patience with your child. However, never go overboard with insincere or unrealistic praise. It has been said that helpful praise occurs in two stages.

First, the adult describes with appreciation what he or she sees or feels. Second, after hearing these descriptions with no value judgments (good or bad), children can begin to internally feel the joy of praising themselves.

One mother said to her 4-year-old, after he brought home a crayon drawing from preschool, "Teddy, you are a great painter. I'll bet it was the best one in the class." Although most children won't really believe such exaggeration, those that do may learn to expect the same kind of response from not only their teachers but from the world at large. More appropriate comments would be, "Teddy likes to draw with the color green," "You like to make circles and triangles," or "Daddy feels good looking at your drawing." The message to Teddy will be that he can draw whatever he likes, and he can decide if he likes it. Teddy learns to praise himself.

Attitude Is Everything

HAVING THE right attitude is an essential aspect in helping maintain a healthy dialogue with your toddler or child. Your mood as well as style of communication tells your child whether you are calm, explosive, or impulsive. This is what your child will see and learn as his or her example of how to manage frustration and conflict. Life experience teaches us that when we manage our emotions in a healthy way we become more centered and calm. Why am I emphasizing this so much? It is the backdrop for all our communication and behavior.

I am reminded of the story of a sixth-grade school teacher who always started the school year by asking the children, "How do you want to be when you grow up?" Invariably, hands would fly in the air and the kids would say, "I want to be a fireman." "I want to be a race car driver." The teacher would pause and say, "Kids, that's not what I asked. I asked how do you want to be, not what do you want to do. Do you want to help people; do you want to be kind, thoughtful, or generous?" This very insightful teacher understood that a healthy attitude will reflect healthy values.

Four Ways to Improve Your Attitude

Sometimes parents ask, "How can I improve my attitude in my relationship with my child? How can I be lighter, more relaxed, and more patient?" This is a big question, and it gets to the heart of how to live life more fully and happily in general.

Here are some practical ideas to think about that can make a dramatic difference in helping you improve your parenting attitude:

> Having the right attitude is an essential aspect in helping maintain a healthy dialogue with your toddler or child. Your mood as well as style of communication tells your child whether you are calm, explosive, or impulsive. This is what your child will see and learn as his or her example of how to manage frustration and conflict.

1. Begin by doing more reading about what you can expect developmentally from your child now and over the next few years. This will help prepare you to be more realistic. Being realistic will reduce your anxiety and expectations. Good books, parent groups, and talking with healthy families are a good way to learn about what to expect. (Haim Ginott's book *Between Parent and Child* is a good place to start.)

2. In addition to reading new materials, don't forget about your own instincts and common sense. Remember, you have more experience than you think. After all, you were once a child! You just need to relax and remember those feelings. One of the joys and surprises of parenthood is the way children help us get in touch with ourselves.

3. Temper what many people have to say about your children and parenting style. Their disappointments, frustrations, and unfortunate failures are not yours. Don't be scared by their stories; rather, be inspired by your instincts. The fact that you are drawn to books like this one already reveals that you are way ahead of those critics.

4. Surround yourself, to the extent you can, with people who project positive attitudes and healthy families. Look for people who push themselves to grow and change. Spending too much time with people who are generally negative and complain about the world can drag anyone into a morose mood.

*A great teacher once said that
the three keys to happiness are
attitude, timing, and laughter.*

10

Sugarcoating "No's"

SOMETIMES WE THINK it helps to call a child a cute name when we have to tell them "no." "Sweetheart, honey . . . no. We have to go now." Somehow we feel doing so softens the bad news. This is rarely comforting for the child and more likely encourages resistance. Although the parent is trying to be loving and understanding, it's usually heard as begging and apologizing from the child's point of view. When a parent means business and the limit has been exceeded, parents need to issue a firm command. "Tommy, 5 minutes have passed. It's time to go. I expect you to walk with me now."

In other more relaxed instances, most parents feel good about calling their toddler cutesy names (Bumkin, Pumpkin, Honey, etc.). At first blush these names sound innocuous, but on closer examination you will see how these innocent expressions of love do nothing to promote your child's sense of self and maturity. This is not to suggest that those parents who prefer to call their children pet names (unless they are degrading names) are doing any sort of psychological damage to their children. They're not.

However, if the goal is to advance and strengthen your child's identity, then the limiting of pet names in favor of his or her *own* name will encourage that process. For the first five years, your child's name should be said almost every time you talk with them. Just as there is no limit on how many times you can pick up an infant without spoiling him, there is no limit on how many times you can call your child by his real name. Hearing their name helps children feel their identity and reinforces their autonomy. After all, they just came into the world a short while ago. Remember all those books and advice you consulted trying to come up with the right name? Remember the first time you saw your baby and thought, "Wow, he really fits his name"? So why do so many parents call their children so many different names? "Munchkin!" "Butterball!" "Slugger!" "Monkey!" We should try to limit using pet names for our children during their early years. A study I once read revealed that a majority of parents call their infant, toddler, or child by their own name less than 50 percent of the time each day. I was curious about this and informally conducted my own survey with about 200 mothers. I asked if they called their child by a "pet name" about half the time each day. I found my results to be the same.

Cute names can be confusing and can also promote jealousy, as other people in and out of the family are often called by the same common pet name. "Sweetheart, there's someone on the phone." "Honey, you look so pretty." However, when you are talking to your child and saying, "Aaron, would you like to read this book?" or "Dana, look at these pictures," your child knows you are talking to her and only her! A child learns her name by being called by it and feeling good about hearing it often.

Silly Names Can Hurt

ONE LITTLE boy I met whose name was Bobby was convinced that he also had a second name: Bob-e-Boo. He would hear throughout the day his mother say, "Bob-e-Boo, time to come in." Other parents—with great love in their hearts—unwittingly use degrading pet names such as "my little monkey," or "my little monster" when they talk to their child. Ironically, these are the same names a 5-year-old will call his playmate when he becomes frustrated and angry! As a child gets older and grasps the meaning behind the pet name, sometimes he carries that image and those feelings with him. One 38-year-old mother still remembers her father calling her "little stinky." She remembers getting that name when she was 4 years old. Her underpants were soiled with a strong odor, and her father would repeatedly laugh, saying, "Wow, that was a stinky. You're my little stinky!" If parents are honest with themselves, they could probably recall more than a few times when they felt embarrassed or degraded by someone calling them a silly name. If you can remember, so will your child. Leontine Young, a pioneering social worker of her time, once said, "The smaller the person, the less we worry about his dignity. Sometimes we even find the idea a little ludicrous, as if smallness and inexperience were incompatible with anything so majestic as human dignity. . . . Yet children have a great sense of their own dignity. They couldn't define what it is but they know when it has been violated."

> If parents are honest with themselves, they could probably recall more than a few times when they felt embarrassed or degraded by someone calling them a silly name. If you can remember, so will your child.

Silly Names Can Make a Child Act Like a Baby

Your attitude and tone in how you say your child's real name can be far more pleasing and loving to your child than any pet name.

In addition, you will encourage more mature behavior. Every time you talk baby talk to a child, you're encouraging infant or baby behavior. Indeed, many children hearing these nicknames will act out the kind of characterization implied by the pet name more readily. These expressions are in direct conflict with a child's natural development and desire to be independent from Mommy, Daddy, and other family members.

The results of this conflict can sometimes be observed later in life, when adults who are not so secure with their own identity resist ever being called by a nickname. They may feel disrespected or become antagonistic when called by one, no matter how endearing. For example, I once witnessed a waitress ask a customer, "Sweetie, can I get you something else?" and his terse reply was "Yes . . . another waitress!"

When a child hears his name said respectfully, it continues to influence how he feels about himself.

11

A Matter of Trust

Building trust with your child is based on the same principles used for building trust with a friend, a peer at work, or a spouse. It's based on truth, consistent forthrightness, protection, and action steeped in faith. Although these may seem like weighty issues for dealing with everyday parent-child communication, they are, nonetheless, what defines a healthy parenting approach.

Children have the capacity to be extremely resilient and responsible when information is shared with them in an honest way. For the most part, they intuitively know when they're being misled or manipulated. Those times when they initially believe that you're telling them the truth and later find out differently, they almost always forgive—but it becomes harder to forget. Although it's not popular to say so, the true test of a child's trust in you can be gauged by how many times your toddler or child abides by what you say.

Many of today's popular psychology books will try to convince you that long periods (3 to 5 months) of acting out, tantrums, and general rowdy behavior are normal for children and just a stage. Of course, to some extent this behavior *is* natural. To a larger extent, it's a symptom of conflict. Whenever possible, avoid using tricks or deception when you want your child to do something or when you're explaining an action. Tricks can be insignificant gestures used to distract, such as telling your child to try some "rice" when it is really beans. Or, perhaps you tell him you can't play with him because you're not feeling well and then he later sees you being very active in the house. If you try to deceptively distract him from something he is really interested in rather than dealing with his curiosity directly, you may be only fooling yourself. The early social worker Leontine Young has concluded that there are only two reasons why any child decides to give up something he wants to do or does something he doesn't like. One reason is fear and punishment, which become the enforcer. The other reason is the wish to please someone important, and love is the enforcer. Normally in everyday life, both necessarily find their place.

The important question to ask, then, is which motive predominates and becomes the prime determiner of behavior? When it is fear, the rules of the outside and the power of the enforcer tell the story. In other words, a child's own sense of right or wrong may give way to someone of authority or to someone bigger and stronger. When it is love, self-discipline builds the structure of consciousness and self-examination. Once again we return to the fundamental concept of how important the right words are: "David, I know you'll do the right thing," or "Jackie, I know you know better." Conveying a confidence in children that they will behave correctly (even if they don't) will have positive long-term results. Many of the popular child psychology books on the market today discuss the different "tricks" parents can use to get kids to do what they want, techniques in "reverse psychology," or games designed to distract—all designed to help parents cope. The problem with this kind of thinking is that it originates from a negative attitude toward respecting what your child is really thinking and from a philosophy of deceit in trying to fool him. The irony here is that though the child is rarely fooled, the parents actually think that what they did worked!

Don't Fool Yourself

LET'S LOOK at a true story. One little boy, almost 2 years old, began asking his mother each·time she changed him if he could look at his bowel movement. The mother, not knowing how to deal with his request, would say, "No, it's not for Richie to play with." Of course, Richie never asked to play with his bowel movement—he just wanted to look at it. Richie became angry and fussed on the changing table, making it almost impossible for his mother to change him.

By the second day, diaper changing had become a very stressful experience for both Richie and Mom. That afternoon, Richie's mother went to her local bookstore, found a book on "the terrible two's," and read about a technique under the heading "Tricks That Work." The next morning Richie needed a change and once again asked to see his bowel movement. Richie's mother put her new advice to work by pacifying and distracting. She immediately lied to Richie, saying, "Later, yes, later we will look at it," and then immediately turned on the cassette player in his room and began singing his favorite song. To make a long story short, her strategy worked! For the next week she pacified and distracted Richie during changing, and he never asked again. Richie's mother was so happy she had learned how to cope that she forgot about her son's feelings. But you can be sure that Richie didn't forget. He will remember and feel three things:

> My curiosity is not important.
> My questions aren't important.
> I'm not important!

Richie's mother had completely trivialized his feelings and what was on his mind. Though it is true that toddlers and children often just act silly, they still prefer to be taken seriously while learning and having fun. So although tricking your toddler or using clever ploys might sometimes get you results, it is done at a very high price.

Constant negative criticism and threats directed toward your toddler or child will encourage him to respond in one of two ways: He will continue to rebel, or he will submit and obey out of fear and intimidation. If your child obeys, you may think you're parenting well, but don't fool yourself. What you may be lacking is his trust. When your toddler or child continues to ignore what you say, that is proof of this cumulative lack of trust. In order to win back his trust, acknowledge his feelings, taking your time when you talk. "Andy is angry and Daddy understands. We will come back later and visit with all your friends. We will come in the same car and take the same roads to get here." Your cadence should be even and the ideas easy to follow. Try to resist the temptation to talk faster and introduce more complicated themes. Often parents are convinced that their child "gets it," thereby talking faster. Remember that children equate time with trust.

> Though it is true that toddlers and children often just act silly, they still prefer to be taken seriously while learning and having fun. So although tricking your toddler or using clever ploys might sometimes get you results, it is done at a very high price.

A classic tale by Charles Dickens carries a good message for parents. *A Christmas Carol* teaches us it is impossible to relive our yesterdays, thus emphasizing the meaning of our deeds today. There comes a time when we, like Ebenezer Scrooge, must look at ourselves as others see us and, more importantly, as our children see us.

Sometimes it's hard to see that we are doing something harmful when, in our hearts, we think we're doing something good. Parents may think they are displaying great wisdom in their teachings, yet at times they are systematically robbing their toddler of his precious spirit. "Larry, no. How many times do I have to tell you not to do that?" "No, Susan, let me do that for you."

Other times parents may abruptly preempt a potential misbehavior at the expense of the child's opportunity to regulate himself. The parent will intrude too soon with a watchful sound of "Na, na, na." This signals a lack of confidence from the parent and implies that the child can't stop himself. Even if you know he will transgress, it is better to allow him to transgress than to interfere. Children will notice your respect for their choice of behavior. In the long run this will continue to strengthen their conscience and ability to self-regulate, and in the short run they will accept the consequences faster and with less struggle because they know the behavior was their choice.

As in any relationship that is being established on trust, one person must trust first. In the case of parenting, the parent always offers his or her faith and trust first. Eddie was 5 years old when he told his father, "No, I won't let Carol use my new computer game! If you make me do it, when you leave the room I'll take it back!" His father said, "I don't think you will." "Why?" asked Eddie. His father replied, "I trust you, Eddie. You will make the right decision." In this manner, Eddie's father clearly conveyed the message, I respect you; I trust you; I have confidence in my son Eddie to do the right thing.

Trust is a process that builds day by day.
Trusting a child builds his conscience.
A child will learn to trust when
he doesn't feel judged.

12

"Say It Again"

I F A PARENT doesn't possess the patience to practice the art of repetition, a child will not learn quickly or in the correct way. Each day when you talk with your toddler, do you often repeat the same words or teach the same lessons 20 times with an attitude that reflects understanding and kindness? If the answer is "yes," then you are on the road to demonstrating solid patience. The literal definition of repetition is "repeating; doing again; saying again." A child's lack of performance and motivation can be directly tied to a lack of repetition shown him. Ralph Waldo Emerson once said, "Nature is an endless combination of repetition of a very few laws." You know this principle to be true when you learn a foreign language, practice a sport, or learn a musical instrument. Those that repeat and repeat and repeat will excel.

All parents will agree they want to teach their children how to be patient, self-motivated, moral, and compassionate. Though they won't always agree on the methods used to teach those lessons, most will agree on the importance of using repetition as a teaching tool. So then why do many parents start out calm as they explain to their toddler his or her misbehavior, only to lose their patience and start yelling just minutes later? Why do parents irrationally believe that teaching a toddler self-control can be achieved in a day or a few weeks?

As an adult, you know in your heart how many hundreds of chances you give yourself to improve your own emotional balance.

Be patient with your child; allow him to work it out so later he won't act it out! It might surprise you to learn that it's never boring or exhausting for the child to hear the same answer over and over again. Indeed, repetition, when given with respect, makes him feel more relaxed and secure with himself and his world.

Intuitively, most of us know that there are no 5-minute remedies for anything worthwhile. Still, we irrationally accept the Madison Avenue marketing propaganda that tells us we can achieve powerful results in 5 minutes. As parents and educators, we must resist these campaigns and return to what we intuitively know will work.

Nothing Works in 5 Minutes

CHILDREN AS well as toddlers look and wait for inconsistencies in their parents' behavior. They do this to test their parents' ability to maintain or extend the limit. Part of the reason parents are inconsistent with their children is due to their own inconsistencies with themselves. In short, sometimes we don't know how to say "no" to our children because sometimes we can't say "no" to ourselves.

We live in an age of instant information. We demand immediate satisfaction. There seems to be no time to reflect, only to react. Everyone wants everything in minutes: fast food, photos, toned bodies, business success, even love relationships. Intuitively, most of us know that there are no 5-minute remedies for anything worthwhile. Still, we irrationally accept the Madison Avenue marketing propaganda that tells us we can achieve powerful results in 5 minutes. As parents and educators, we must resist these campaigns and return to what we intuitively know will work. There is no shortcut for the emotional process. You can't expect to do something once and have it work immediately.

Not much of anything worthwhile can be accomplished in 5 minutes. It may take 5 months of employing the strategies outlined in this book before you begin to see consistent results. Considering the stakes—nothing short of your child's emotional development—that kind of time passes in the blink of an eye.

13

Summary
of "Know's"

THE CONCEPT THAT infants, toddlers, and children possess far more understanding than we often acknowledge is not new. Yet some parents' actions reveal that they often ignore this fact. We see this when parents talk about their children, right in front of them, as though they're not present.

It is not my intention with this book to address why parents do what they do. My goal is to provide parents with practical solutions to allow them to see alternate ways of communicating and building trust with their children. I hope I've shattered some of the myths about what are considered "normal phases or problems" of child development, replacing them with commonsense solutions that limit childhood repression and allow for expression and learned self-control.

Teaching a child to emotionally adjust to her environment is no longer thought to be an automatic process, but a learned behavior. Psychologist and author Daniel Goleman dispels the 1960s myth that the IQ is the most important factor in determining the success and happiness of an individual. He argues and scientifically supports the theory that "emotional intelligence," which includes self-control, persistence, temperament, and the ability to motivate oneself, can be taught. According to Goleman, "These skills will give [children] a better chance to use their intellectual potential the genetic lottery may have given them at birth." His model of what it means to be intelligent puts emotions at the center of aptitudes for living.

At times it can feel overwhelming trying to remember everything we read or hear that appeals to our better senses about parenting. However, as a rule, if you ever lose your bearings, just ask yourself, "Am I talking with respect? Do I allow my child the freedom to express all his feelings?" It cannot be overstated that the center of aptitudes for parenting is the mutual trust and respect between the parent and child.

Tips for Communicating with Your Infant

BEFORE WE interfere with our infant's freedom and mobility, let's remember that saying "no" too frequently can diminish enthusiasm and curiosity. Don't make a moment an event. Their rite of passage for the first 15 months is all about exploration and discovering their experimental powers. Early impulses to crawl in a clear direction are the first signs of self-motivation.

Tips for Communicating with Your Toddler and Older Child

- Toddlers and children may not always obey, but they almost always listen. Choose your words thoughtfully. This is critical in building mutual trust and respect.

- Remember, the mind manifests itself. Concentrate on your child's behavior, not his intelligence.

- Stop all the baby talk. Talk up to your toddler, not down.

- Help shape her identity. Call her by her real name, not a pet name.

- Don't talk about your child in front of him.

- When you need to correct your child, don't humiliate.

- Try not to teach your child the value of sharing before the age of 2. Rather, teach children about their emotions by reflecting their feelings and their actions: "You want to play with the toy by yourself," or "I can tell you're angry at me."

- Don't just reprimand with a "no." Remember to say, "I know you know better." This will promote self-confidence.

- Don't just issue "no" commands—give your child choices.

> At times it can feel overwhelming trying to remember everything we read or hear that appeals to our better senses about parenting. However, as a rule, if you ever lose your bearings, just ask yourself, "Am I talking with respect? Do I allow my child the freedom to express all his feelings?"

- Keep your own emotions in check. If a child feels right, he acts right. When he does transgress, try to maintain your own self-control. That's what they'll be watching! That's how they'll ultimately learn self-control.

- Never ignore or discount a child's feelings or fantasies. Never say, "You don't mean that." Instead say, "Sounds like you're your pretty angry at Sam," or "You mean you wish you never had to see Grandma again."

- Always allow for the expression of feelings. As Dr. Ginott said, "Birds fly, fish swim, and children feel." That doesn't mean you allow all behavior. It does mean you allow all feelings.

Be your child's example of what the right behavior looks and sounds like. Be sincere. Be authentic. Be respectful.

Children Will Listen

Careful the things you say—
children will listen.
Careful the things you do—
children will see
and learn.
Children may not obey
but children will listen.
Children will look to you
for which way to turn,
to learn what to be.
Careful before you say,
"Listen to me."
Children will listen.

How do you say to your child in the night,
"Nothing's all black, but then
nothing's all white?"
How do you say, "It will be all right"
when you know that it mightn't be true?
What do you do?

Careful the wish you make—
wishes are children.
Careful the path they take—
wishes come true,
not free.
Careful the spell you cast,
not just on the children.
Sometimes the spell may last

past what you can see
and turn against you . . .
Careful the tale you tell:
that is the spell.
Children will listen.

Music and lyrics by Stephen Sondheim
Sung by Mandy Patinkin from his CD *Oscar and Steve*

Appendix:
Key Concepts at a Glance

The 7-Step Method for Saying "No"

Be sincere, empathetic, and firm as you go through this process with your child. Keep repeating and emphasize the choice at the end.

1. Confirm the request. "Yes, Alex, you want to go outside." (say twice)
2. Give facts. "It's raining. The paper plane will get wet and the wings will be too heavy to fly." (say twice)
3. Affirm feelings. "I know you're feeling angry. I see you're mad at me." (say twice)
4. Allow in fantasy what you can't in reality. "You wish it would stop raining so we could play outside. You wish it was bright and sunny outside. I wish it were, too!" (say twice)
5. Demonstrate (when possible). "Look Alex, feel the rain outside." (open the door and show your child, twice) "Look what happens when the paper plane gets wet."
6. Give confidence. "I know you understand, Alex." (say twice or more with your child's name)
7. Give choices. "You can play in your room or stay in the kitchen. The choice is yours. You make the choice." (say twice)

5 Reasons Why Giving Facts Works Better Than Saying the Word "No"

1. Allows the child to reason and come to his own answers and conclusions.
2. Takes the focus away from the perception and feeling that the parent is being unfair and heavy-handed.
3. Does not make the parent the messenger of the word no.
4. Shows respect for the child's ability to understand.
5. Reduces feelings of resentment from the child.

Don't Just "Go" . . . "Visit"

We teach that we *visit* parks but can't take home the rides. We *visit* our friends homes and don't take home their furniture and toys. Why can't we *visit* a store without feeling compelled to buy something?

Just before it's time to go to the store remember to remind your two-year-old you will only be visiting not buying. Then ask her, "Let me hear you say you understand." When leaving the store give your child few minutes of advance notice—sometimes several times—so he can begin to prepare himself. You say, "Tommy, we have to go in three minutes."

When the time is up you say, "Our visiting time is up, it's time to leave. Tommy, we have to go now, we're visiting . . . we're just visiting. I know you understand. We will come back and visit soon. Everything will be waiting for you." (Pause and wait for response.) If he is holding a toy, say "I know you wish you could take that racecar with you. You wish you could take the whole store with you. Today we are visiting. Now it's time to leave." After about three or four months of calling these trips *visits,* your child's response will become more positive and trusting. The word *visit* reinforces the concept that sharing, playing, and going somewhere does not mean *getting* something.

Preparing Your Child to Leave
When the Time Is Up

1. Give an advance notice of time. Adults as well as children do not like to be abruptly stopped in the middle of something fun or interesting. Giving advance notice about when something will happen shows your child you value his time as well as your own. It also allows him time to prepare for accepting his "limit."

2. By repeating the theme of *visiting*, you put the emphasis on exactly that part of the experience and begin to establish a different future expectation.

3. By giving your child in fantasy what he can't have in reality ("I wish you could take the racecar with you"), you are showing him understanding. This diminishes his anger and encourages cooperation.

4. Allow and accept all your child's feelings by reflecting back to him how he is feeling.

5. Remember, slow and sincere repetition is critical to the communication process. It will also help your toddler to relax.

4 Reasons Why "I Know You Understand" Works Better Than "No"

Be sure you have explained your reasons and have confidence that your child understands what you have said before you say "I know you understand."

1. You are expressing respect for your child since you are telling him you know that he knows better.
2. It allows him to think about his misbehavior without the fear of punishment. This will help develop his conscience.
3. You're telling him he has the intelligence to understand.
4. You have the confidence in him to correct the misbehavior.

Bibliography

Ames, Louise, Frances L. Ilg, and Carol C. Haber. *Your Two-Year-Old.* Gesell Institute. New York: Dell, 1976.

Axline, Virginia. *Dibs: In Search of Self.* New York: Ballantine, 1969.

Baruch, Dorothy. *New Ways in Discipline.* New York: McGraw-Hill, 1949.

Elkind, David. *The Hurried Child.* Massachusetts: Addison-Wesley, 1981.

Eyre, Linda, and Richard Eyre. *Teaching Your Children Values.* New York: Simon & Schuster, 1993.

Faber, Mazlish. *How to Talk So Kids Will Listen & Listen So Kids Will Talk.* New York: Avon, 1980.

———. *Liberated Parents, Liberated Children.* New York: Avon, 1974.

Fraiberg, Selma. *The Magic Years.* New York: Macmillan Publishing, 1959.

Ginott, Haim. *Between Parent and Child.* New York: Avon, 1969.

———. *Between Parent and Teenager.* New York: Avon, 1969.

———. *Teacher and Child.* New York: Avon, 1975.

Glasser, William. *The Quality School Teacher.* New York: HarperCollins, 1993.

Goleman, Daniel. *Emotional IQ.* New York: Bantam, 1995.

Greenspan, Stanley. *First Feelings.* New York: Viking Penguin, 1985.

———. *Playground Politics.* Massachusetts: Addison-Wesley, 1993.

Guerney, Louise F. *Parenting: A Skills Training Manual.* Nashville: Ideals, 1995.

Holt, John. *How Children Fail.* New York: Pitman Publishing, 1968.

Kraft, Arthur. *Parents as Therapeutic Partners: Listening to Your Child's Play.* Jason Aronson, 1998

Mahler, Margaret, Fred Pine, and Anni Bergman. *The Psychological Birth of the Human Infant.* New York: Basic Books, 1975.

Miller, Alice. *The Drama of the Gifted Child.* New York: Basic Books, 1981.

Nagel, Greta. *The TAO of Teaching.* New York: Donald I. Fine, 1994.

Landreth, Garry. *Parents as Therapeutic Partners: Listening to Your Child's Play.* Jason Aronson, 1998.

Piaget, Jean. *The Origins of Intelligence in Children.* Paris: Delachaux & Niestle, 1936.

———. *Science of Education and the Psychology of the Child.* Paris: Orion, 1969.

Rosemond, John. *Six-Point Plan for Raising Happy, Healthy Children.* Kansas City: Andrews and McMeel, 1989.

Shimm, Patricia, and Kate Ballen. *Parenting Your Toddler.* Massachusetts: Addison-Wesley, 1995.

Stern, Daniel. *Interpersonal World of the Infant.* New York: Basic Books, 1985.

Index

Learn to Love Your Child the Right Way

Parents Who Love Too Much explores the issue of parents who, in an effort to be good, conscientious parents, end up either indulging or over-protecting their children. Bestselling authors Jane Nelsen and Cheryl Erwin explore this cultural shift in thinking and offer practical solutions for parents who can't figure out why they've lost their kid's respect in the process. Parents will learn:

- **Why protecting children from all discomfort stifles their emotional growth**
- **How parents can empathize without rescuing**
- **How to parent with long-term goals in mind**
- **How to set limits and say "no" without feeling guilty**
- **And much more!**

"One of the ironies of parenting is that unwise love can harm children. This book will help you apply your love more intelligently and beneficially."
—RICHARD EYRE, author of the #1 *New York Times* bestseller *Teaching Your Children Values*

PARENTS WHO LOVE TOO MUCH

How Good Parents Can Learn to Love More Wisely and Develop Children of Character

FROM THE AUTHORS OF THE MILLION-COPY SELLING POSITIVE DISCIPLINE SERIES
JANE NELSEN, ED.D.
CHERYL ERWIN, M.A.

ISBN 0-7615-2142-9
Paperback / 336 pages
U.S. $16.95 / Can. $25.95

Available everywhere books are sold.
Visit us online at www.primapublishing.com.

PRIMA